WILEY SERIES 9
SECURITIES LICENSING
EXAM REVIEW 2020
+ TEST BANK

WILEY SECURITIES LICENSING SERIES

This series includes the following titles:

Wiley Securities Industry Essentials Exam Review 2020

Wiley Series 3 Securities Licensing Exam Review 2020 + Test Bank: The National Commodities Futures Examination

Wiley Series 4 Securities Licensing Exam Review 2020 + Test Bank: The Registered Options Principal Examination

Wiley Series 6 Securities Licensing Exam Review 2020 + Test Bank: The Investment Company and Variable Contracts Products Representative Examination

Wiley Series 7 Securities Licensing Exam Review 2020 + Test Bank: The General Securities Representative Examination

Wiley Series 9 Securities Licensing Exam Review 2020 + Test Bank: The General Securities Sales Supervisor Examination—Option Module

Wiley Series 10 Securities Licensing Exam Review 2020 + Test Bank: The General Securities Sales Supervisor Examination—General Module

Wiley Series 24 Securities Licensing Exam Review 2020 + Test Bank: The General Securities Principal Examination

Wiley Series 26 Securities Licensing Exam Review 2020 + Test Bank: The Investment Company and Variable Contracts Products Principal Examination

Wiley Series 57 Securities Licensing Exam Review 2020 + Test Bank: The Securities Trader Examination

Wiley Series 63 Securities Licensing Exam Review 2020 + Test Bank: The Uniform Securities Agent State Law Examination

Wiley Series 65 Securities Licensing Exam Review 2020 + Test Bank: The Uniform Investment Adviser Law Examination

Wiley Series 66 Securities Licensing Exam Review 2020 + Test Bank: The Uniform Combined State Law Examination

Wiley Series 99 Securities Licensing Exam Review 2020 + Test Bank: The Operations Professional Examination

For more on this series, visit the website at www.securitiesCE.com.

WILEY SERIES 9 SECURITIES LICENSING EXAM REVIEW 2020 + TEST BANK

The General Securities
Sales Supervisor
Examination—Option Module

The Securities Institute of America, Inc.

WILEY

Contents

CHAPTER 5
OPTION TAXATION AND MARGIN REQUIREMENTS 93

CHAPTER 6
OPTION COMPLIANCE AND ACCOUNT SUPERVISION 102

About the Series 9 Exam

Congratulations! You are on your way to becoming a Series 9 general securities sales supervisor, registered to supervise a member firm's option business. The Series 9 exam will be presented in a 55-question multiple-choice format. Each candidate will have one hour and 30 minutes to complete the exam. A score of 70% or higher is required to pass on both the Series 9 and Series 10 portions to become fully registered as a general securities sales supervisor.

The Series 9 is as much a knowledge test as it is a reading test. Your textbook and software from The Securities Institute will ensure that you have the required knowledge to pass the test and that you are confident in the application of that knowledge during the exam. The writers and instructors at The Securities Institute are subject-matter experts as well as Series 9 test experts. We understand how the test is written, and our proven test-taking techniques can dramatically improve your results.

 IMPORTANT EXAM NOTE

The Series 9 exam may use the terms FINRA, NASD, or both to describe itself or its rules. Test takers are advised to be aware of this and to treat the two terms as interchangeable. This text in most instances uses the most up-to-date term—FINRA.

TAKING THE SERIES 9 EXAM

The Series 9 exam is presented in multiple-choice format on a touch-screen computer known as the PROCTOR system. No computer skills are required, and candidates will find that the test screen works in the same way as an ordinary ATM machine. Each test is made up of 55 questions that are randomly chosen from a test bank of thousands of questions. Each Series 9 exam will have several practice questions that do not count toward the final score. The test has a time limit of 1 hour and 30 minutes and is designed to provide enough time for all candidates to complete the exam. In addition to passing the Series 9 Option Module, each candidate must pass the Series 10 General Securities Sales Supervisor General Module.

The Series 9 exam will be composed of 55 questions relating to options and option regulations.

HOW TO PREPARE FOR THE SERIES 9 EXAM

It is recommended that the candidate spend 30 to 40 hours preparing for the exam by reading the textbook, underlining key points, and by taking as many practice questions as possible.

Test-Taking Tips

☐ Read the full question before answering.

☐ Identify what the question is asking.

☐ Identify key words and phrases.

☐ Watch out for hedge clauses, such as *except* and *not*.

☐ Eliminate wrong answers.

☐ Identify synonymous terms.

☐ Be wary of changing answers.

WHAT TYPE OF BUSINESS MAY BE CONDUCTED BY SERIES 9 REGISTERED REPRESENTATIVES?

After passing the Series 9 exam, a registered person may supervise a member firm's option business.

WHAT SCORE IS NEEDED TO PASS THE EXAM?

A score of 70% or higher is needed to pass the Series 9 exam.

ARE THERE ANY PREREQUISITES FOR THE SERIES 9?

The Series 7 is a prerequisite of the Series 9 exam. The Series 10 is a corequisite for a person to be fully registered as a general securities sales supervisor for a member firm.

HOW DO I SCHEDULE AN EXAM?

Ask your firm's principal to schedule the exam for you or to provide a list of test centers in your area. In most states, you must be sponsored by a FINRA member firm prior to making an appointment. The Series 9 exam may be taken any day that the exam center is open.

WHAT MUST I BRING TO THE EXAM CENTER?

A picture ID is required. All other materials will be provided, including a calculator and scratch paper.

HOW LONG WILL IT TAKE TO GET THE RESULTS OF THE EXAM?

The exam will be graded as soon as you answer your final question and hit the Submit for Grading button. It will take only a few minutes to get your results. Your grade will appear on the computer screen, and you will be given a paper copy at the exam center.

If you do not pass the test, you will need to wait 30 days before taking it again. If you do not pass on the second try, you will need to wait another 30 days. If you fail a third time, you must wait 6 months to take the test again.

About This Book

The writers and instructors at The Securities Institute have developed the Series 9 textbook, exam prep software, and videos to ensure that you have the knowledge required to pass the test and to make sure that you are confident in the application of that knowledge during the exam. The writers and instructors at The Securities Institute are subject-matter experts as well as Series 9 test experts. We understand how the test is written, and our proven test-taking techniques can dramatically improve your results.

Each chapter includes notes, tips, examples, and case studies with key information, hints for taking the exam, and additional insight into the topics. Each chapter ends with a practice test to ensure that you have mastered the concepts before moving on to the next topic.

About the Test Bank

This book is accompanied by a test bank of more than 150 questions to further reinforce the concepts and information presented here. The access card in the back of this book includes the URL and PIN code you can use to access the test bank. This test bank provides a small sample of the questions and features that are contained in the full version of the Series 9 exam prep software.

If you have not purchased the full version of the exam prep software with this book, we highly recommend that you do so to ensure that you have mastered the knowledge required for your Series 9 exam. To purchase the exam prep software for this exam, visit The Securities Institute of America online at www.SecuritiesCE.com or call 877-218-1776.

About The Securities Institute of America

The Securities Institute of America, Inc. helps thousands of securities and insurance professionals build successful careers in the financial services industry every year.

Our securities training options include:

- Classroom training.
- Private tutoring.
- Interactive online video training classes.
- State-of-the-art exam preparation software.
- Printed textbooks.
- Real-time tracking and reporting for managers and training directors.

As a result, you can choose a securities training solution that matches your skill level, learning style, and schedule. Regardless of the format you choose, you can be sure that our securities training courses are relevant, tested, and designed to help you succeed. It is the experience of our instructors and the quality of our materials that make our courses requested by name at some of the largest financial services firms in the world.

To contact The Securities Institute of America, visit us on the Web at www.SecuritiesCE.com or call 877-218-1776.

Option Basics

INTRODUCTION

An option is a contract between two parties that determines the time and price at which a stock may be bought or sold. The two parties to the contract are the buyer and the seller. The buyer of the option pays money, known as the option's premium, to the seller. For this premium, the buyer obtains a right to buy or sell the stock depending on what type of option is involved in the transaction. Because the seller has received the premium from the buyer, the seller now has an obligation to perform under that contract. Depending on the option involved, the seller may have an obligation to buy or sell the stock.

OPTION CLASSIFICATION

Options are classified as to their type, class, and series. There are two types of options: calls and puts.

OPTION TYPES

CALL OPTIONS

A call option gives the buyer the right to buy, or to "call," the stock from the option seller at a specific price for a certain period of time. The sale of a call option obligates the seller to deliver or sell that stock to the buyer at that specific price for a certain period of time.

PUT OPTIONS

A put option gives the buyer the right to sell, or to "put," the stock to the seller at a specific price for a certain period of time. The sale of a put option obligates the seller to buy the stock from the buyer at that specific price for a certain period of time.

OPTION CLASSES

An option class consists of all options of the same type for the same underlying stock.

EXAMPLE

All XYZ calls are one class of options, and all XYZ puts are another class of options.

Class 1	Class 2
XYZ June 50 calls	XYZ June 50 puts
XYZ June 55 calls	XYZ June 55 puts
XYZ July 50 calls	XYZ July 50 puts
XYZ July 55 calls	XYZ July 55 puts
XYZ August 50 calls	XYZ August 50 puts

OPTION SERIES

An option series is the most specific classification of options and consists only of options of the same class with the same exercise price and expiration month. For example, all XYZ June 50 calls would be one series of options, and all XYZ June 55 calls would be another series of options.

BULLISH VS. BEARISH

BULLISH

Investors who believe that a stock price will increase over time are said to be bullish. Investors who buy calls are bullish on the underlying stock; that is, they believe that the stock price will rise and have paid for the right to purchase the stock at a specific price known as the exercise price or strike price. An investor who has sold puts is also considered to be bullish on the stock. The seller of a put has an obligation to buy the stock and, therefore, believes that the stock price will rise.

BEARISH

Investors who believe that a stock price will decline are said to be bearish. The seller of a call has an obligation to sell the stock to the purchaser at a specified price and believes that the stock price will fall and is therefore bearish. The buyer of a put wants the price to drop so that he or she may sell the stock at a higher price to the seller of the put contract and is also considered to be bearish.

	Calls	Puts
Buyers	Bullish	Bearish
	Have right to buy stock, want stock price to rise	Have right to sell stock, want stock price to fall
Sellers	Bearish	Bullish
	Have obligation to sell stock, want stock price to fall	Have obligation to buy stock, want stock price to rise

BUYER VS. SELLER

Buyer		Seller
Owner	Known as	Writer
Long	Known as	Short
Rights	Has	Obligations
Maximum speculative profit	Objective	Premium income
With an opening purchase	Enters the contract	With an opening sale
Exercise	Wants the option to	Expire

POSSIBLE OUTCOMES FOR AN OPTION

EXERCISED

If the option is exercised, the buyer has elected to exercise the right to buy or sell the stock, depending on the type of option involved. Exercising an option obligates the seller to perform under the contract.

SOLD

Most individual investors will elect to sell their rights to another investor rather than exercise their rights. The investor who buys the option will acquire all the rights of the original purchaser.

EXPIRE

If the option expires, the buyer has elected not to exercise the right, and the seller of the option is relieved of the obligation to perform.

EXERCISE PRICE

The exercise price is the price at which an option buyer may buy or sell the underlying stock, depending on the type of option involved in the transaction. The exercise price is also known as the strike price.

CHARACTERISTICS OF ALL OPTIONS

All standardized option contracts are issued and their performance is guaranteed by the Options Clearing Corporation (OCC). Standardized options trade on the exchanges, such as the Chicago Board Options Exchange (CBOE) and the NYSE Alternext.

All option contracts are for one round lot of the underlying stock, or 100 shares. To determine the amount that an investor either paid or received for the contract, take the premium and multiply it by 100. If an investor paid $4 for 1 KLM August 70 call, the investor paid $400 for the right to buy 100 shares of KLM at $70 per share until August. If another investor paid $2 for 1 JTJ May 50 put, the investor paid $200 for the right to sell 100 shares of JTJ at $50 until May.

MANAGING AN OPTION POSITION

Both the buyer and seller, in an option trade, establish the position with an opening transaction. The buyer has an opening purchase, and the seller has an opening sale. To exit the option position, an investor must close out the position. The buyer of the option may exit a position through:

- A closing sale.
- Exercising the option.
- Allowing the option to expire.

The seller of an option may exit or close out a position through:

- A closing purchase.
- Having the option exercised or assigned.
- Allowing the option to expire.

Most individual investors do not exercise their options and will simply buy and sell options in much the same way as they would buy or sell other securities.

BUYING CALLS

An investor who purchases a call believes that the underlying stock price will rise and that he or she will be able to profit from the price appreciation by purchasing calls. An investor who purchases a call can control the underlying stock and profit from its appreciation while limiting the loss to the amount of the premium paid for the calls. Buying calls allows investors to maximize their leverage, and they may realize a more significant percentage return based on their investment. An investor may also elect to purchase a call to lock in a purchase price for a security if the investor currently lacks the funds required to purchase the security but will have the funds available in the near future. When looking to establish a position, buyers must determine:

- Their maximum gain.
- Their maximum loss.
- Their breakeven.

MAXIMUM GAIN FOR A LONG CALL

When an investor has a long call position, the maximum gain is always unlimited. The investor profits from a rise in the stock price. Because there is no limit to how high a stock price may rise, the maximum gain is unlimited just as if the investor had purchased the stock.

MAXIMUM LOSS FOR A LONG CALL

Whenever an investor is long, or owns a stock, the maximum loss is always limited to the amount that has been invested. When an investor purchases a call option, the amount paid for the option, or the premium, is always going to be the maximum loss.

BREAKEVEN POINT FOR A LONG CALL

An investor who has purchased calls must determine where the stock price must be at expiration in order to break even on the transaction. An investor who has purchased calls has paid the premium to the seller in the hopes that the stock price will rise. The stock must appreciate by enough to cover the cost of the investor's option premium in order for the investor to break even at expiration. To determine an investor's breakeven point on a long call, use the following formula:

$$\text{breakeven} = \text{strike price} + \text{premium}$$

| EXAMPLE | An investor has established the following option position: Long 1 XYZ May 30 call at 3. The investor's maximum gain, maximum loss, and breakeven will be: |

- Maximum gain: Unlimited
- Maximum loss: $300 (premium paid)
- Breakeven: $33 = 30 + 3 (strike price + premium)

If at expiration XYZ is at exactly $33 per share and the investor sells or exercises the option, the investor will break even, excluding transaction costs.

SELLING CALLS

An investor who sells a call believes that the underlying stock price will fall and that he or she will be able to profit from a decline in the stock price by selling calls. An investor who sells a call is obligated to deliver the underlying stock if the buyer decides to exercise the option. When looking to establish a position, sellers must determine:

- Their maximum gain.
- Their maximum loss.
- Their breakeven.

MAXIMUM GAIN FOR A SHORT CALL

For an investor who has sold uncovered or naked calls, the maximum gain is always limited to the amount of the premium received when the calls were sold.

MAXIMUM LOSS FOR A SHORT CALL

An investor who has sold uncovered or naked calls does not own the underlying stock and, as a result, has unlimited risk and the potential for an unlimited loss. The seller of the calls is subject to a loss if the stock price increases. Because there is no limit to how high a stock price may rise, there is no limit to the amount of investor's loss.

BREAKEVEN POINT FOR A SHORT CALL

An investor who has sold calls must determine where the stock price must be at expiration in order to break even on the transaction. An investor who has sold calls has received the premium from the buyer in the hopes that the stock price will fall. If the stock appreciates, the investor may begin to lose money. The stock price may appreciate by the amount of the option premium received, and the investor will still break even at expiration. To determine an investor's breakeven point on a short call, use the following formula:

breakeven = strike price + premium

EXAMPLE

An investor has established the following option position: Short 1 XYZ May 30 call at 3. The investor's maximum gain, maximum loss, and breakeven will be:

- Maximum gain: $300 (premium received)
- Maximum loss: Unlimited
- Breakeven: $33 = 30 + 3 (strike price + premium)

If at expiration XYZ is at exactly $33 per share and the investor closes out the transaction with a closing purchase or has the option exercised against him or her, the investor will break even, excluding transaction costs.

Notice the relationship between the buyer and the seller:

	Call Buyer	**Call Seller**
Maximum gain	Unlimited	Premium received
Maximum loss	Premium paid	Unlimited
Breakeven	Strike price + premium	Strike price + premium
Wants option to	Exercise	Expire

Because an option is a two-party contract, the buyer's maximum gain is the seller's maximum loss, and the buyer's maximum loss is the seller's maximum gain. Both the buyer and the seller will break even at the same point.

BUYING PUTS

An investor who purchases a put believes that the underlying stock price will fall and that he or she will be able to profit from a decline in the stock price by purchasing puts. An investor who purchases a put can control the underlying stock and profit from its price decline while limiting his or her loss to the amount of the premium paid for the puts. Buying puts allows investors to maximize their leverage while limiting their losses. It may also allow investors to realize a more significant percentage return based on their investment compared to the return that could be realized from shorting stock. When looking to establish a position, buyers must determine:

- Their maximum gain.
- Their maximum loss.
- Their breakeven.

MAXIMUM GAIN FOR A LONG PUT

An investor who has purchased a put believes that the stock price will fall. There is, however, a limit to how far a stock price may decline. A stock price may never fall below zero. As a result, the investor who believes that the stock price will fall has a limited maximum gain. To determine the maximum gain for the buyer of a put, use the following formula:

maximum gain = strike price − premium

MAXIMUM LOSS FOR A LONG PUT

Whenever an investor is long, or owns a stock, the maximum loss is always limited to the amount invested. When investors purchase a put option, the amount they pay for the option, or their premium, is always going to be their maximum loss.

BREAKEVEN FOR A LONG PUT

An investor who has purchased a put believes that the stock price will decline. In order for the investor to break even on the transaction, the stock price must fall by enough to offset the amount of the premium paid for the option. At expiration, the investor will break even at the following point:

breakeven = strike price – premium

EXAMPLE	An investor has established the following option position: Long 1 XYZ May 30 put at 4. The investor's maximum gain, maximum loss, and breakeven will be:

- Maximum gain: $26, or $2,600 for the whole position (strike price – premium)
- Maximum loss: $400 (premium paid)
- Breakeven: $26 = 30 − 4 (strike price – premium)

If at expiration XYZ is at exactly $26 per share and the investor sells or exercises the option, the investor will break even, excluding transactions costs.

SELLING PUTS

An investor who sells a put believes that the underlying stock price will rise and that he or she will be able to profit from a rise in the stock price by selling puts. An investor who sells a put is obligated to purchase the underlying stock if the buyer decides to exercise the option. An investor who sells a put may also be selling the put as a way to acquire the underlying security at a cheaper price. If the stock is put to the investor, the investor's purchase price is reduced by the amount of the premium received. When looking to establish a position, sellers must determine:

- Their maximum gain.
- Their maximum loss.
- Their breakeven.

MAXIMUM GAIN FOR A SHORT PUT

For an investor who has sold uncovered or naked puts, the maximum gain is always limited to the amount of the premium the investor received when he or she sold the puts.

MAXIMUM LOSS FOR A SHORT PUT

An investor who has sold a put believes that the stock price will rise. There is, however, a limit to how far a stock price may decline. A stock price may never fall below zero. As a result, the investor who believes that the stock price will rise has a limited maximum loss. The worst thing that can happen for an investor who is short a put is that the stock goes to zero and the investor is then forced to purchase it at the strike price from the owner of the put. To determine the maximum loss for the seller of a put, use the following formula:

maximum loss = strike price – premium

BREAKEVEN FOR A SHORT PUT

Whenever an investor has sold a put, he or she believes that the stock price will rise. If the stock price begins to fall, the investor becomes subject to a loss. In order for the investor to break even on the transaction, the stock price may fall by the amount of the premium received for the option. At expiration, the investor will break even at the following point:

breakeven = strike price – premium

EXAMPLE	An investor has established the following option position: Short 1 XYZ May 30 put at 4. The investor's maximum gain, maximum loss, and breakeven will be:

- Maximum gain: $400 (premium received)
- Maximum loss: $26, or $2,600 for the whole position (strike price – premium)
- Breakeven: $26 = 30 – 4 (strike price – premium)

If at expiration XYZ is at exactly $26 per share and the investor closes out the position with a closing purchase or has the option exercised against him or her, the investor will break even, excluding transaction costs.

Notice the relationship between the buyer and the seller:

	Put Buyer	Put Seller
Maximum gain	Strike price – premium	Premium received
Maximum loss	Premium paid	Strike price – premium
Breakeven	Strike price – premium	Strike price – premium
Wants option to	Exercise	Expire

Because an option is a two-party contract, the buyer's maximum gain is the seller's maximum loss, and the buyer's maximum loss is the seller's maximum gain. Both the buyer and the seller will break even at the same point.

OPTION PREMIUMS

The price of an option is known as its premium. Factors that determine the value of an option and, as a result, its premium, are:

- The relationship of the underlying stock price to the option's strike price.
- The amount of time to expiration.
- The volatility of the underlying stock.
- Supply and demand.
- Interest rates.

An option can be:

- In the money.
- At the money.
- Out of the money.

These terms describe the relationship of the underlying stock to the option's strike price. These terms do not describe how profitable the position is.

IN THE MONEY OPTIONS

A call is in the money when the underlying stock price is greater than the call's strike price.

EXAMPLE   An XYZ June 40 call is $2 in the money when XYZ is at $42 per share.

A put is in the money when the underlying stock price is lower than the put's strike price.

EXAMPLE   An ABC October 70 put is $4 in the money when ABC is at $66 per share.

It would only make sense to exercise an option if it was in the money.

AT THE MONEY OPTIONS

Both puts and calls are at the money when the underlying stock price equals the options exercise price.

EXAMPLE   If FDR is trading at $60 per share, all of the FDR 60 calls and all of the FDR 60 puts will be at the money.

OUT OF THE MONEY OPTIONS

A call is out of the money when the underlying stock price is lower than the option's strike price.

EXAMPLE   An ABC November 25 call is out of the money when ABC is trading at $22 per share.

A put option is out of the money when the underlying stock price is above the option's strike price.

EXAMPLE   A KDC December 50 put is out of the money when KDC is trading at $54 per share.

It would not make sense to exercise an out of the money option.

	Calls	Puts
In the money	Stock price > strike price	Stock price < strike price
At the money	Stock price = strike price	Stock price = strike price
Out of the money	Stock price < strike price	Stock price > strike price

INTRINSIC VALUE AND TIME VALUE

An option's total premium is composed of intrinsic value and time value. An option's intrinsic value is equal to the amount the option is in the money. Time value is the amount by which an option's premium exceeds its intrinsic value. In effect, the time value is the price an investor pays for the opportunity to exercise the option. An option that is out of the money has no intrinsic value; therefore, the entire premium consists of time value.

EXAMPLE   An XYZ June 40 call is trading at $2 when XYZ is trading at $37 per share. The June 40 call is out of the money and has no intrinsic value; therefore, the entire $2 premium consists of time value. If an XYZ June 40 put is trading at $3 when XYZ is at $44 dollars per share, the entire $3 is time value.

If in the above example, the options were in the money and the premium exceeded the intrinsic value of the option, the remaining premium would be time value.

EXAMPLE   An XYZ June 40 call is trading at $5 when XYZ is trading at $42 per share. The June 40 call is in the money and has $2 in intrinsic value; therefore, the rest of the premium consists of the time value of $3. If an XYZ June 40 put is trading at $4 when XYZ is at $39, the put is in the money by $1, and the rest of the premium, or $3, is time value.

Pretest

OPTION BASICS

1. You sold 10 IBM May 95 puts at 5.70. What is your maximum gain?

   a. $570

   b. $5,700

   c. Unlimited

   d. $95,000

2. An investor sells 2 ZAQ Nov 60 puts at 3.5 when ZAQ is at 62.70. ZAQ falls to 56.05 at expiration, and the investor closes the position at its intrinsic value. What is the investor's gain or loss?

   a. $90 profit

   b. $90 loss

   c. $45 loss

   d. $45 profit

3. Which of the following are true about an option?

    I. It is a contract between two parties that determines the time and place at which a security may be bought or sold.

    II. The two parties are known as the buyer and the seller. The money paid by the buyer of the option is known as the option's premium.

    III. The buyer has bought the right to buy or sell the security, depending on the type of option.

    IV. The seller has an obligation to perform under the contract, possibly to buy or sell the stock, depending on the option involved.

    a. I, III, and IV

    b. I, II, III, and IV

    c. I, II, and III

    d. II, III, and IV

4. Which of the following are bearish?

    I. Call seller

    II. Put seller

    III. Call buyer

    IV. Put buyer

    a. II and III

    b. II and IV

    c. I and IV

    d. I and II

5. Which of the following issues standardized options?

    a. The exchanges

    b. The OCC

    c. The company

    d. Nasdaq

6. An investor buys 10 XYZ May 70 calls at 3.10 when XYZ is at 68. At expiration, the stock is at 77, and the investor closes out the position at its intrinsic value. What is the investor's profit or loss?

    a. $7,000 profit

    b. $7,000 loss

    c. $3,100 loss

    d. $3,900 profit

7. A MSFT June 65 put trading at 3 has how much intrinsic value with MSFT at 65?

    a. $0

    b. $3

    c. $65

    d. $2

8. With XYZ trading at 52.50, which of the following options is in the money?

    a. XYZ March 55 call

    b. XYZ March 55 put

    c. XYZ March 50 put

    d. XYZ March 60 call

9. An XYZ May 50 call is quoted at 4.35 when XYZ is at 51.10. Which of the following are true?

    I. The time value is 1.10.

    II. The option is in the money.

    III. The time value is 3.25.

    IV. The intrinsic value is more than the time value.

    a. II and III

    b. I and IV

    c. II and IV

    d. I and III

10. An investor sells 10 CSC Oct 75 puts at 5.30 to open. CSC trades down to 71 at expiration, and the investor closes out the position at intrinsic value with a closing purchase. What is the investor's gain or loss?

    a. $1,300 loss
    b. $1,300 gain
    c. $300 loss
    d. $300 gain

Option Strategies

INTRODUCTION

Many investors will use options to manage risk or to establish more complex positions than simply directionally trading options by buying or selling puts and calls. In this chapter, we will review option hedging strategies as well as how and why to establish multiple option positions.

USING OPTIONS AS A HEDGE

Many investors will use options to hedge a position that they have established in the underlying stock. Options can be used to guard against a loss or to protect a profit the investor has in a position. Options, in this case, will operate like an insurance policy for the investor.

LONG STOCK LONG PUTS/MARRIED PUTS

An investor who is long stock and wishes to protect the position from downside risk will receive the most protection by purchasing a protective put. By purchasing the put, the investor has locked in or set a minimum sale price that he or she will receive in the event of the stock's decline for the life of the put. The minimum sale price in this case is equal to the strike price of the put. Long puts can be used with long stock to guard against a loss or to protect an unrealized profit. However, by purchasing the put, the investor has increased the breakeven point by the amount of the premium paid to purchase the put. When looking to establish a long stock long put position, investors must determine:

- Their maximum gain.
- Their breakeven.
- Their maximum loss.

MAXIMUM GAIN FOR A LONG STOCK LONG PUT

An investor who is long stock and long puts has an unlimited maximum gain, because the investor owns the stock.

BREAKEVEN FOR A LONG STOCK LONG PUT

To determine an investor's breakeven for a long stock long put position, you must add the option premium to the cost of the stock:

breakeven = stock price + premium

EXAMPLE   An investor establishes the following position:

Long 100 XYZ at 55.
Long 1 XYZ June 55 put at 3.

The investor will break even if the stock goes to $58. The stock price has to appreciate by enough to offset the amount of the premium that the investor paid for the option. If at expiration the stock is at $58 per share and the put expires, the investor will have broken even, excluding transaction costs.

MAXIMUM LOSS FOR A LONG STOCK LONG PUT

In order to determine an investor's maximum loss when they have established a long stock long put position, you must first determine the breakeven point, as outlined above. Once you have determined the breakeven, use the following formula:

maximum loss = breakeven − strike price

Let's take another look at the previous example, only this time we will use it to determine the investor's maximum loss.

EXAMPLE	Long 100 XYZ at 55.
	Long 1 XYZ June 55 put at 3.

We have already determined that the investor will break even if the stock goes to $58. To determine the investor's maximum loss, we subtract the put's strike price from the investor's breakeven point as follows:

58 − 55 = 3

The investor's maximum loss is $3 per share, or $300 for the entire position. Notice that the option's premium is the investor's maximum loss. When the purchase price of the stock and the strike price of the put are the same, the investor's maximum loss is equal to the premium paid for the option.

Let's take a look at another example where the investor's purchase price is different from the strike price of the put.

EXAMPLE	An investor establishes the following position:

Long 100 XYZ at 58.

Long 1 XYZ June 55 put at 2.

In order to find the investor's maximum loss, we first need to determine the breakeven point. This investor will break even if the stock goes to $60, which is found by adding the stock price to the premium the investor paid for the put. To find the maximum loss, we subtract the put's strike price from the breakeven point.

60 − 55 = 5

The investor's maximum loss on this position is $5 per share, or $500 for the entire position.

An investor who is long stock and long puts has limited the potential losses and has received the maximum possible protection while retaining all of the appreciation potential.

LONG STOCK SHORT CALLS/COVERED CALLS

Investors who are long stock can receive some partial downside protection and generate some additional income by selling calls against the stock they own. Investors will receive downside protection or will hedge their position by the amount of the premium received from the sale of the calls. Although this results in partial downside protection, the investor will give up any appreciation potential above the call's strike price. Investors who wish to establish a covered call position must determine:

- Their breakeven.
- Their maximum gain.
- Their maximum loss.

BREAKEVEN POINT FOR A LONG STOCK SHORT CALL

By selling the calls, the investor has lowered the breakeven on the stock by the amount of the premium received from the sale of the calls. To determine the investor's breakeven in this case, the price to which the stock can fall, use the following formula:

purchase price of the stock − premium received

EXAMPLE   An investor establishes the following position:

Long 100 ABC at 65.

Short 1 ABC June 65 call at 4.

Using the formula above, we get:

65 − 4 = 61

The stock price in this case can fall to $61, and the investor will still break even.

MAXIMUM GAIN FOR A LONG STOCK SHORT CALL

Because investors have sold call options on the stock that they own, they have limited the amount of their gain. Any appreciation of the stock beyond the call's strike price belongs to the investor who purchased the call. To determine an investor's maximum gain on a long stock short call position, use the following formula:

maximum gain = strike price − breakeven

Let's use the same example to determine the investor's maximum gain.

EXAMPLE

Long 100 ABC at 65.

Short 1 ABC June 65 call at 4.

Using the formula above, we get:

65 − 61 = 4

The investor's maximum gain is $4 per share, or $400 for the entire position. Notice that because the purchase price of the stock and the strike price of the call are the same, the investor's maximum gain is equal to the amount of the premium received on the sale of the call.

Let's look at an example where the strike price and the purchase price for the stock are different.

EXAMPLE

An investor establishes the following position:

Long 100 ABC at 65.

Short 1 ABC June 70 call at 2.

The investor will break even at $63, which is found by subtracting the premium received from the investor's purchase price for the stock. To determine the investor's maximum gain, subtract the breakeven from the strike price:

70 − 63 = 7

The investor's maximum gain is $7 per share, or $700 for the entire position.

MAXIMUM LOSS FOR A LONG STOCK SHORT CALL

An investor who has sold covered calls has only received partial downside protection in the amount of the premium received. As a result, the investor is still subject to a significant loss in the event of an extreme downside move in the stock price. To determine an investor's maximum loss for long stock short calls, use the following formula:

maximum loss = breakeven − 0

Said another way, an investor is subject to a loss equal to the breakeven price per share.

EXAMPLE

An investor establishes the following position:

Long 100 ABC at 65.
Short 1 ABC June 70 call at 2.

The investor will break even at $63, found by subtracting the premium received from the investor's purchase price for the stock. To determine the investor's maximum loss, we only need to look at the breakeven point and we get a maximum loss of $63 per share, or $6,300 for the entire position. The investor will realize the maximum loss if the stock goes to zero.

RATIO CALL WRITING

An investor who is long stock may elect to write calls covering more shares than the investor owns. As a result, the investor will have written both covered calls and uncovered calls. This is known as ratio writing. For example, an investor may elect to write calls in a 2:1, 3:1, or 4:1 ratio. The investor will realize the greatest gain if the stock is stable and the options expire. The investor will have an unlimited potential loss as a result of the naked or uncovered calls.

 TAKENOTE!

The investor's account must be approved for uncovered options prior to executing any ratio writing or overwriting strategy.

SHORT STOCK LONG CALLS

Investors who sell stock short believe that they can profit from a fall in the stock price by selling it high and repurchasing it cheaper. An investor who has sold stock short is subject to an unlimited loss if the stock price should begin to rise. Once again, there is no limit to how high a stock price may rise. An investor who has sold stock short would receive the most protection by purchasing a call. A long call could be used to guard against a loss or to protect a profit on a short stock position. By purchasing the call, the investor has set the maximum price that he or she will have to pay to repurchase the stock for the life of the option. Before establishing a short stock long call position, investors will have to determine:

- Their breakeven.
- Their maximum gain.
- Their maximum loss.

BREAKEVEN POINT FOR A SHORT STOCK LONG CALL

An investor who has sold stock short will profit from a fall in the stock price. When an investor has purchased a call to protect a position, the stock price must fall by enough to offset the premium the investor paid for the call. To determine the breakeven for a short stock long call position, use the following formula:

breakeven = stock price − premium

EXAMPLE	An investor establishes the following position:

Short 100 ABC at 60.

Long 1 ABC October 60 call at 2.

Using the above formula, we get:

60 − 2 = 58

The stock would have to fall to $58 by expiration in order for the investor to break even.

MAXIMUM GAIN FOR A SHORT STOCK LONG CALL

The maximum gain on the short sale of stock is always limited because a stock cannot fall below zero. When an investor has a short stock long call position, the maximum gain is found by using the following formula:

maximum gain = breakeven − 0

Said another way, the investor's maximum gain per share would be equal to the breakeven price per share. Let's return to our example from above.

EXAMPLE

Short 100 ABC at 60.

Long 1 ABC October 60 call at 2.

Using the formula above, we get:

58 − 0 = 58

If the stock fell to $0 by expiration, the investor would realize a maximum gain of $58 per share, or $5,800 for the entire position.

MAXIMUM LOSS FOR A SHORT STOCK LONG CALL

An investor who has sold stock short and has purchased a call to protect a position is only subject to a loss up to the strike price of the call. In order to determine the investor's maximum loss, use the following formula:

maximum loss = strike price − breakeven

EXAMPLE

Short 100 ABC at 60.

Long 1 ABC October 60 call at 2.

Using the formula above, we get:

60 − 58 = 2

The investor is subject to a loss of $2 per share, or $200 for the entire position. Notice that the price at which the investor sold the stock short and the strike price of the call are the same. As a result, the investor has set a maximum repurchase price equal to the price at which the investor sold the stock short.

The investor's maximum loss when the sale price and strike price are the same is the amount of the premium that the investor paid for the call. Let's take a look at a position where the sale price of the stock and strike price of the option are different.

EXAMPLE

An investor establishes the following position:

Short 100 ABC at 56.

Long 1 ABC October 60 call at 2.

This investor will break even at $54 per share. To determine the investor's maximum loss, subtract the breakeven point from the strike price of the option:

60 − 54 = 6

The investor is subject to a loss of $6 per share, or $600 for the entire position.

SHORT STOCK SHORT PUTS

An investor who has sold stock short can receive some protection and generate premium income by selling puts against the short stock position. Selling puts against a short stock position will only partially hedge the unlimited upside risk associated with any short sale of stock. Additionally, the investor, in exchange for the premium received for the sale of the put, has further limited the maximum gain. Before entering a short stock short put position, investors must determine:

- Their breakeven.
- Their maximum gain.
- Their maximum loss.

BREAKEVEN FOR A SHORT STOCK SHORT PUT

An investor who has sold stock short and sold puts against the position is subject to a loss if the stock price begins to rise. To determine how high a stock price could rise after establishing a short stock short put position and still allow the investor to break even, use the following formula:

breakeven = stock price + premium

EXAMPLE	An investor establishes the following position:

Short 100 ABC at 55.
Short 1 ABC November 55 put at 4.

Using the formula above, we get:

55 + 4 = 59

In this case, the stock could rise to $59 by expiration and still allow the investor to break even excluding transaction costs.

MAXIMUM GAIN FOR A SHORT
STOCK SHORT PUT

An investor who has established a short stock short put position has limited the amount of gain even further by selling puts, because the investor will be required to purchase the shares at the put's strike price if the stock declines. To determine the investor's maximum gain, use the following formula:

maximum gain = breakeven − strike price

EXAMPLE   An investor establishes the following position:

Short 100 ABC at 55.
Short 1 ABC November 55 put at 4.

The investor will break even at 59, which is found by adding the stock price of 55 and the option premium of 4 together. Using the above formula, we get:

59 − 55 = 4

The investor's maximum gain in this case is $4 per share, or $400 for the entire position. The investor received a total of $59 per share by establishing the position. If the stock fell to zero, the investor would still be required to repurchase the shares at 55 under the terms of the put contract. Notice that the sales price and the put's exercise price are the same and the amount of the investor's maximum gain is equal to the amount of the premium received.

Let's look at a position where the sale price of the stock and the strike price of the put are different.

EXAMPLE   An investor establishes the following position:

Short 100 XYZ at 60.
Short 1 XYZ November 55 put at 4.

The investor will break even at 64. To determine the investor's maximum gain using the formula above, we get:

64 − 55 = 9

The investor's maximum gain is $9 per share, or $900 for the total position.

MAXIMUM LOSS FOR A SHORT STOCK SHORT PUT

An investor who has sold puts against a short stock position has only limited the possible loss by the amount of the premium received from the sale of the put. As a result, the investor's loss in a short stock short put position is still unlimited.

Underlying Position	Most Protection	Some Protection & Income
Long stock	Long puts	Short calls
Short stock	Long calls	Short puts

 TAKE**NOTE!**

It's important to note that investors that want the most protection are going to buy the hedge. Investors that want some protection as well as income will sell the hedge.

MULTIPLE OPTION POSITIONS AND STRATEGIES

Option strategies that contain positions in more than one option can be used effectively by investors to meet their objectives and to profit from movement in the underlying stock price.

LONG STRADDLES

A long straddle is the simultaneous purchase of a call and a put on the same stock with the same strike price and expiration month. An option investor would purchase a straddle when he or she expects the stock price to be extremely volatile and to make a significant move in either direction. An investor who owns a straddle is neither bullish nor bearish. The investor is not concerned with whether the stock moves up or down in price, so long as it moves significantly. An investor may purchase a straddle just prior to a company announcing earnings, with the belief that if the company beats its earnings estimate the stock price will appreciate dramatically or if the company's earnings fall short of expectations the stock price will decline dramatically. Before establishing a long straddle, investors must determine the following:

- Their maximum gain
- Their maximum loss
- Their breakeven

Let's look at an example.

EXAMPLE   XYZ is trading at $50 per share and is set to report earnings at the end of the week. An investor with the above opinion establishes the following position:

Long 1 XYZ April 50 call at 4.

Long 1 XYZ April 50 put at 3.

MAXIMUM GAIN FOR A LONG STRADDLE

Because the investor in a long straddle owns the calls, the investor's maximum gain is always going to be unlimited.

MAXIMUM LOSS FOR A LONG STRADDLE

An investor's maximum loss on a long straddle is going to be limited to the total premium paid for the straddle. The total premium is found using the following formula:

total premium = call premium + put premium

EXAMPLE   XYZ is trading at $50 per share and is set to report earnings at the end of the week. An investor establishes the following position:

Long 1 XYZ April 50 call at 4.

Long 1 XYZ April 50 put at 3.

To determine the investor's maximum loss, simply add the premiums together.

$4 + 3 = 7$

The investor's maximum loss is $7 per share, or $700 for the entire position. The investor will only realize the maximum loss on a long straddle if the stock price at expiration is exactly equal to the strike price of both the call and put and both options expire worthless. If, at expiration, XYZ closes at exactly $50, the investor in this case will suffer the maximum possible loss.

BREAKEVEN FOR A LONG STRADDLE

Because the position contains both a put and a call, the investor is going to have two breakeven points, one for the call side of the straddle and one for the put side. To determine the breakeven point for the call side of the straddle, use the following formula:

breakeven = call strike price + total premium

EXAMPLE

XYZ is trading at $50 per share and is set to report earnings at the end of the week. An investor establishes the following position:

Long 1 XYZ April 50 call at 4.

Long 1 XYZ April 50 put at 3.

The total premium is 7. Therefore:

50 + 7 = 57

The investor will break even if XYZ appreciates to $57 per share at expiration. The stock has to appreciate by enough to offset the total premium cost.

Alternatively, to determine the breakeven point for the put side of the straddle, use the following formula:

breakeven = put strike price − total premium

50 − 7 = 43

If XYZ was to fall to $43 per share at expiration, the investor would break even. The stock would have to fall by enough to offset the total premium cost. If the stock appreciated past $57 per share or fell below $43 per share, the position would become profitable for the investor.

 FOCUSPOINT

An investor who is long a straddle wants the stock price outside of the breakeven points. In our example, that would be either above $57 per share or below $43 per share.

SHORT STRADDLES

A short straddle is the simultaneous sale of a call and a put on the same stock with the same strike price and expiration month. An option investor would sell a straddle when he or she expects the stock price to trade within a narrow range or to become less volatile and not to make a significant move in either direction. An investor who is short a straddle is neither bullish nor bearish. The investor is not concerned with whether the stock moves up or down in price, so long as it does not move significantly. An investor may sell a straddle just after a period of high volatility, with the belief that the stock will now move sideways for a period of time. Before establishing a short straddle, investors must determine the following:

- Their maximum gain
- Their maximum loss
- Their breakeven

MAXIMUM GAIN FOR A SHORT STRADDLE

An investor's maximum gain with a short straddle is always going to be limited to the amount of the premium received. Let's look at the same position from before; only this time, let's look at it from the seller's point of view.

EXAMPLE

XYZ is trading at $50. An option investor establishes the following position:

Short 1 XYZ April 50 call at 4.

Short 1 XYZ April 50 put at 3.

To determine the investor's maximum gain, simply add the premiums together.

$$4 + 3 = 7$$

The investor's maximum gain is $7 per share, or $700 for the entire position. An investor who is short a straddle will only realize the maximum gain if the stock closes at the strike price at expiration and both options expire worthless. In this case, if XYZ closes at exactly $50, the investor will have a $700 profit on the entire position.

MAXIMUM LOSS FOR A SHORT STRADDLE

Because the investor in a short straddle is short the call, the investor's maximum loss is always going to be unlimited.

BREAKEVEN FOR A SHORT STRADDLE

Just like with a long straddle, the investor is going to have two breakeven points, one for the call side of the straddle and one for the put side. To determine the breakeven point for the call side of the straddle, use the following formula:

breakeven = call strike price + total premium

EXAMPLE

XYZ is trading at $50. An option investor establishes the following position:

Short 1 XYZ April 50 call at 4.

Short 1 XYZ April 50 put at 3.

The total premium is 7. Therefore, using the above formula:

50 + 7 = 57

The investor will break even if XYZ appreciates to $57 per share at expiration.

Alternatively, to determine the breakeven point for the put side of the straddle, use the following formula:

breakeven = put strike price − total premium

50 − 7 = 43

If XYZ was to fall to $43 per share at expiration, the investor would break even. If the stock appreciated past $57 per share or fell below $43 per share, the investor would begin to lose money.

 FOCUSPOINT

An investor who is short a straddle wants the stock price inside of the breakeven points. In the above case, that would be either below $57 per share or above $43 per share.

Position	Maximum Gain	Maximum Loss	Breakeven	At Expiration
Long straddle	Unlimited	Total premium	Strike price + or − total premium	Profitable if outside breakeven
Short straddle	Total premium	Unlimited	Strike price + or − total premium	Profitable if inside breakeven

TESTTIP!

To remember where an investor wants the stock to be at expiration, use the mnemonic device for straddles: SILO, short inside long outside.

SELLING A STRADDLE AGAINST LONG STOCK

An investor may also elect to sell a straddle against a long stock position. This will result in more premium income and more risk to the investor than selling a covered call. An investor who sells a straddle against an underlying stock position ends up with a covered call and a naked put. If the stock falls, the investor could be forced to purchase additional shares of the stock because of the short put. This magnifies the investor's downside risk for the entire position. To determine an investor's breakeven for a long stock short straddle position, use the following formula:

$$\frac{\textbf{stock price} + \textbf{strike price} - \textbf{premium received}}{2}$$

EXAMPLE

An investor purchased 100 shares of XYZ at 49 and sells 1 XYZ July 50 call for 2 and sells one XYZ June 50 put for 3. Using the formula above, we get:

$$\frac{49 + 50 - 5}{2} = 94/2 = 47$$

The investor will break even if the stock falls to 47. At any point below 47 the investor is losing money, and at any point above 47 the investor is making money. Because the investor sold the call, the investor has also limited the upside potential gain.

SPREADS

A spread is created through the simultaneous purchase and sale of two options of the same class with different exercise prices, expiration months, or both. Several different types of spreads may be created using either calls or puts, including the following:

- Price spread/vertical spread/money spread
- Calendar spread/time spread/horizontal spread
- Diagonal spread

PRICE SPREAD/VERTICAL SPREAD

A price spread or vertical spread consists of one long option and one short option of the same class with different strike prices. The position is normally called a price spread because of the difference in strike prices between the long and short options. It may also be called a vertical spread because of the way the options are listed in the option chain or in the newspaper. A price spread could be established in either calls or puts.

EXAMPLE   A price spread can be established with calls:

Long 1 TRY May 40 call.
Short 1 TRY May 50 call.

A price spread can also be established using puts:

- Long 1 TRY April 60 put.
- Short 1 TRY April 50 put.

CALENDAR SPREAD/TIME SPREAD

A calendar spread or time spread contains one long option and one short option of the same class with different expiration months. It may also be called a horizontal spread because of how the options are listed in the option chain or in the newspaper.

EXAMPLE   A time spread can be established using calls:

Short 1 TRY June 40 call.
Long 1 TRY August 40 call.

A time spread can also be established using puts:

Short 1 TRY January 60 put.
Long 1 TRY April 60 put.

DIAGONAL SPREAD

A diagonal spread consists of one long option and one short option of the same class that have different strike prices and expiration months. The position is called a diagonal spread because of the way the options are listed in the option chain or in the newspaper.

EXAMPLE   A diagonal spread can be established using calls:

Short 1 TRY June 50 call.
Long 1 TRY August 40 call.

A diagonal spread can also be established using puts:

Short 1 TRY March 40 put.
Long 1 TRY August 50 put.

ANALYZING PRICE SPREADS

Investors who are bullish or bearish can use spreads to profit from their opinion about prices in the marketplace. We will use price spreads to determine:

- If the investor is bullish or bearish.
- If the position has resulted in a net debit or credit.
- The maximum gain.
- The maximum loss.
- The breakeven point.
- If the investor wants the options to be exercised or to expire.
- If the investor wants the difference in the premiums to widen or narrow.

BULL CALL SPREADS/DEBIT CALL SPREADS

To establish a bull call spread, the investor purchases the call with the lower strike price and simultaneously sells the call with the higher strike price. An investor who believes that the stock price will rise may purchase the call with the lower strike price and sell the call with the higher strike price to offset the risk of losing all of the premium paid for the long call. A bull call spread will always be a debit spread because the right to purchase a stock at a lower price for the same amount of time will always be worth more than the right to purchase the same stock at a higher price.

EXAMPLE   A bull call spread could be established as follows:

Long 1 XYZ April 40 call at 3.

Short 1 XYZ April 50 call at 1.

By selling the April 50 call, the investor has reduced his maximum loss from $300 to $200 for the entire position. By selling the April 50 call, the investor has also limited the upside potential on the position.

Before entering into a bull call spread, investors must determine:

- Their maximum gain.
- Their maximum loss.
- Their breakeven.

MAXIMUM GAIN FOR A BULL CALL SPREAD/DEBIT CALL SPREAD

The maximum gain on a bull call spread has been limited because the investor has sold the call with the higher strike price. Any appreciation past the strike price of the short call will belong to the investor who purchased the call. To determine the maximum gain on a bull call spread, use the following formula:

difference in the strike prices – net premium paid

EXAMPLE   An investor has established the following bull call spread:

Long 1 XYZ April 40 call at 3.

Short 1 XYZ April 50 call at 1.

Therefore, based on the formula above we get:

10 – 2 = 8

The investor's maximum gain is $8 per share, or $800 for the entire position. The investor will realize the maximum gain if both options are exercised.

MAXIMUM LOSS FOR A BULL CALL SPREAD/DEBIT CALL SPREAD

An investor who is long a bull call spread has a maximum loss equal to the amount of the net premium paid for the spread. An investor will realize the maximum loss if both options expire worthless at expiration.

BREAKEVEN FOR A BULL CALL SPREAD

To determine where the stock has to be at expiration for the investor to break even, use the following formula:

lower strike price + net premium

EXAMPLE   An investor has established the following bull call spread:

Long 1 XYZ April 40 call at 3.
Short 1 XYZ April 50 call at 1.

Based on the formula above, we get:

40 + 2 = 42

If at expiration XYZ is at $42 per share, the investor will break even on the position, excluding transaction costs. If the stock is higher than $42 per share, the investor will make money. If it is lower than $42, the investor will lose money.

THE SPREAD PREMIUM FOR A BULL CALL SPREAD/DEBIT CALL SPREAD

An investor who has established a bull call spread has bought the spread and paid a net premium to establish the position. The investor will realize a profit on the spread if the difference in the premiums increases or widens. Let's look at our example again.

EXAMPLE   Long 1 XYZ April 40 call at 3.
Short 1 XYZ April 50 call at 1.

The difference between the premium on the long April 40 call and the short April 50 call is 2. If the difference in the value of the premiums increases or widens, the investor will make money.

Let's look at the value of the same spread at expiration given different closing prices for XYZ.

	Opened at	XYZ at 45	XYZ at 50	XYZ at 30
Long 1 XYZ April 40 call	3	5	10	0
Short 1 XYZ April 50 call	1	0	0	0
Difference	2	5	10	0
Profit/loss	N / A	$300	$800	($200)

Notice that the difference between the premiums can never widen past the amount of the spread. This is a 10-point spread; therefore, the difference between the value of the premiums may never widen past 10.

BEAR CALL SPREADS

To establish a bear call spread, the investor sells the call with the lower strike price and simultaneously buys the call with the higher strike price. An investor who believes that the stock price will fall may sell the call with the lower strike price and purchase the call with the higher strike price to ensure that the maximum loss is not unlimited.

EXAMPLE

A bear call spread/credit call spread could be established as follows:

Short 1 XYZ April 40 call at 3.
Long 1 XYZ April 50 call at 1.

Before entering into a bear call spread, investors must determine:

- Their maximum gain.
- Their maximum loss.
- Their breakeven.

MAXIMUM GAIN FOR A BEAR CALL SPREAD

The maximum gain for a bear call spread is equal to the net premium or credit received by the investor when he or she sold the spread.

EXAMPLE

Short 1 XYZ April 40 call at 3.
Long 1 XYZ April 50 call at 1.

The net premium received by the investor is $2 per share, or $200 for the entire position. This amount represents the investor's maximum gain. The investor will realize the maximum gain if both options expire.

MAXIMUM LOSS FOR A BEAR CALL SPREAD

The maximum loss on a bear call spread is limited because the investor bought the call with the higher strike price. If the investor was only short a naked call, the maximum loss would be unlimited. To determine the maximum loss on a bear call spread, use the following formula:

difference in the strike prices − net premium received

EXAMPLE   Short 1 XYZ April 40 call at 3.

Long 1 XYZ April 50 call at 1.

Using the formula above, we get:

10 − 2 = 8

The investor's maximum loss is $8 per share, or $800 for the entire position. The investor will realize the maximum loss if both options are exercised.

BREAKEVEN FOR A BEAR CALL SPREAD

To determine where the stock has to be at expiration for the investor to break even, use the following formula:

lower strike price + net premium

EXAMPLE   Short 1 XYZ April 40 call at 3.

Long 1 XYZ April 50 call at 1.

Using the formula above, we get:

40 + 2 = 42

If at expiration XYZ is at $42 per share, the investor will break even on the position, excluding transaction costs. If the stock is higher than $42 per share, the investor will lose money. If it is lower than $42, the investor will make money.

SPREAD PREMIUM FOR A BEAR CALL SPREAD

An investor who has established a bear call spread has sold the spread and received a net premium or credit to establish the position. The investor will realize a profit on the spread if the difference in the premiums decreases or narrows.

EXAMPLE   Short 1 XYZ April 40 call at 3

Long 1 XYZ April 50 call at 1

The difference between the premium on the short April 40 call and the long April 50 call is 2. If the difference in the value of the premiums decreases or narrows, the investor will make money. Let's look at the value of the same spread at expiration, given different closing prices for XYZ.

	Opened at	XYZ at 45	XYZ at 50	XYZ at 30
Short 1 XYZ April 40 call	3	5	10	0
Long 1 XYZ April 50 call	1	0	0	0
Difference	2	5	10	0
Profit/Loss	N / A	($300)	($800)	$200

Let's compare a bull call spread with a bear call spread:

Position	Maximum Gain	Maximum Loss	Breakeven	At Expiration
Bull call spread	Difference in strike prices – premium paid	Net premium paid	Lower strike price + premium	Profitable if spread widens
Bear call spread	Net premium received	Difference in strike prices – premium received	Lower strike price + premium	Profitable if spread narrows

BEAR PUT SPREADS/DEBIT PUT SPREADS

An investor wishing to profit from a decline in a stock price may establish a bear put spread, also known as a debit put spread. A bear put spread will always be a debit put spread because the right to sell a stock at a higher price is always going to be worth more than the right to sell the same stock at a lower price for the same amount of time. To establish a debit put spread, the investor will purchase the put with the higher strike price and sell the put with the lower strike price. By selling the put with the lower strike price, the investor has reduced the maximum loss by the amount of the premium received.

The investor has also limited the maximum gain, and any profit from the decline of the stock past the lower put's strike price will belong to the investor who purchased the put. Before establishing a bear put spread, investors must determine:

- Their maximum gain.
- Their maximum loss.
- Their breakeven.

MAXIMUM GAIN FOR A BEAR PUT SPREAD/DEBIT PUT SPREAD

The maximum gain for an investor who has established a bear put spread is found by using the following formula:

difference in the strike prices – net premium paid

EXAMPLE   An investor makes the following bear put spread:

> Long 1 XYZ April 50 put at 4
> Short 1 XYZ April 40 put at 1

Using the formula above, we get:

10 − 3 = 7

The investor's maximum gain is $7 per share, or $700 for the entire position. The investor will realize the maximum gain if both options are exercised.

MAXIMUM LOSS FOR A BEAR PUT SPREAD/DEBIT PUT SPREAD

An investor who is long a bear put spread has a maximum loss equal to the amount of the net premium paid for the spread. An investor will realize the maximum loss if both options expire worthless at expiration.

BREAKEVEN FOR A BEAR PUT SPREAD/DEBIT PUT SPREAD

To determine an investor's breakeven point on a bear put spread, use the following formula:

higher strike price − net premium paid

EXAMPLE   Long 1 XYZ April 50 put at 4.
Short 1 XYZ April 40 put at 1.

Using the formula above, we get:

50 − 3 = 47

Therefore, XYZ would have to fall to $47 per share by expiration for the investor to break even. If at expiration XYZ has fallen below $47, the investor will make money. At any point above $47, the investor will lose money.

SPREAD PREMIUM FOR A BEAR PUT SPREAD/DEBIT PUT SPREAD

An investor who has established a bear put spread has bought the spread and paid a net premium to establish the position. The investor will realize a profit on the spread if the difference in the premiums increases or widens.

EXAMPLE

Long 1 XYZ April 50 put at 4.

Short 1 XYZ April 40 put at 1.

The difference between the premiums on the long April 50 put and the short April 40 put is 3. If the difference in the value of the premiums increases or widens, the investor will make money. Let's look at the value of the same spread at expiration, given different closing prices for XYZ.

	Opened at	XYZ at 45	XYZ at 50	XYZ at 30
Long 1 XYZ April 50 put	4	5	0	20
Short 1 XYZ April 40 put	1	0	0	10
Difference	3	5	0	10
Profit/loss	N/A	$200	($300)	$700

BULL PUT SPREADS/CREDIT PUT SPREADS

An investor wishing to profit from a rise in a stock price may establish a bull put spread, which is also known as a credit put spread. A bull put spread will always be a credit put spread, because the right to sell a stock at a higher price is always going to be worth more than the right to sell the same stock at a lower price for the same amount of time. To establish a bull put spread/ credit put spread, the investor would sell the put with the higher strike price and purchase the put with the lower strike price.

EXAMPLE

An investor could profit from a rise in the stock price by establishing a bull put spread as follows:

Short 1 XYZ April 50 put at 4.

Long 1 XYZ April 40 put at 1.

Before establishing a bull put spread, investors need to determine:

- Their maximum gain.
- Their maximum loss.
- Their breakeven.

MAXIMUM GAIN FOR A BULL PUT SPREAD/CREDIT PUT SPREAD

The maximum gain for a bull put spread is equal to the credit received by the investor when he or she sold the spread.

EXAMPLE	Short 1 XYZ April 50 put at 4.
	Long 1 XYZ April 40 put at 1.

The investor received a net credit of $3 per share, or $300 for the entire position. The investor will realize the maximum gain if both options expire.

MAXIMUM LOSS FOR A BULL PUT SPREAD/CREDIT PUT SPREAD

The maximum loss on a bull put spread is found by using the following formula:

difference in the strike prices − net premium received

EXAMPLE	Short 1 XYZ April 50 put at 4.
	Long 1 XYZ April 40 put at 1.

Using the formula from above, we get:

$10 − 3 = 7$

The investor's maximum loss is $7 per share, or $700 for the entire position. The investor will realize the maximum loss if both options are exercised.

BREAKEVEN FOR A BULL PUT SPREAD/CREDIT PUT SPREAD

To determine an investor's breakeven point on a bull put spread, use the following formula:

higher strike price − net premium received

EXAMPLE	Short 1 XYZ April 50 put at 4.
	Long 1 XYZ April 40 put at 1.

Using the formula above, we get:

$50 − 3 = 47$

XYZ could fall to $47 per share by expiration and the investor would still break even. If at expiration XYZ is above $47, the investor will make money. At any point below $47, the investor will lose money.

SPREAD PREMIUM FOR A BULL PUT SPREAD/CREDIT PUT SPREAD

An investor who has established a bull put spread has sold the spread and received a net premium to establish the position. The investor will realize a profit on the spread if the difference between the premiums decreases or narrows. Let's look at our example again.

EXAMPLE	Short 1 XYZ April 50 put at 4.	
	Long 1 XYZ April 40 put at 1.	

The difference between the premiums on the short April 50 put and the long April 40 put is 3. If the difference in the value of the premiums decreases or narrows, the investor will make money. Let's look at the value of the same spread at expiration, given different closing prices for XYZ.

	Opened at	XYZ at 45	XYZ at 50	XYZ at 30
Short 1 XYZ April 50 put	4	5	0	20
Long 1 XYZ April 40 put	1	0	0	10
Difference	3	5	0	10
Profit/loss	N/A	($200)	$300	($700)

Let's compare a bear put spread with a bull put spread.

	Maximum Gain	Max Loss	Breakeven	At Expiration
Bear put spread	Difference in strike prices – premium paid	Net premium paid	Higher strike price – premium	Profitable if spread widens
Bull put spread	Net premium received	Difference in strike prices – premium received	Higher strike price – premium	Profitable if spread narrows

RATIO SPREADS

A ratio spread is established when an investor writes more calls than the investor purchases. The most common ratio is 2:1. An investor may establish a ratio spread as follows:

Buy 1 XYZ May 70 call at 3.
Sell 2 XYZ May 80 calls at 1.

Effectively, the investor has a bull call spread and 1 naked or uncovered call. A ratio spread is also known as a variable spread. Prior to establishing a ratio spread, a customer's account would have to be approved for naked options.

BUTTERFLY SPREADS

A butterfly spread is the simultaneous establishment of both a bull spread and a bear spread on the same underlying security. An investor who establishes a butterfly spread is effectively neutral on the underlying security. A butterfly spread has three option positions: the center strike price and two outer strike prices, or wings (hence the name butterfly spread). The position at the center strike price contains twice the number of contracts as the two outer option positions. An investor establishes a butterfly spread by selling the middle option position and buying the outer wings of the spread. A long butterfly spread is established as a debit spread. Like all debit spreads, the investor's maximum loss will be equal to the net debit paid to establish the position. The investor's maximum gain for the position will be the same as for other spreads: the difference between the strike prices minus the net debit. To determine the maximum gain, use the spread between the center strike price and the outer wings of the spread. A butterfly spread, like a straddle, will have two breakeven points, one above the center strike price and one below. The breakeven point for the upper end of the position will be the higher strike price minus the debit. The breakeven point for the lower end of the position will be the lower strike price plus the debit. A butterfly spread could be established as shown in the following example.

| **EXAMPLE** | An investor establishes the following positions: |

Buy 1 XYZ June 60 call at 3.

Sell 2 XYZ June 50 calls at 6.

Buy 1 XYZ June 40 call at 11.

Debit	Credit
3	12
11	
2	

The investor established the position for a net debit of 2, or $200. Using the formulas described above, we determine that the investor will:

- Have a maximum loss of $200.
- Have a maximum gain of $800 (10-point spread − 2).

- Have a lower breakeven of 42 (lower strike price + debit).
- Have an upper breakeven of 58 (higher strike price – debit)

 TAKENOTE!

An investor would establish a short butterfly if he expected a large move in the price of the underlying security. The seller of the butterfly, like all option sellers, has a maximum gain equal to the net credit received. The seller will realize the maximum gain if the underlying security is above or below the outer strike prices or the wings of the position at expiration.

CONDOR SPREADS

A condor spread is similar to a butterfly spread and is the simultaneous establishment of both a bull spread and a bear spread on the same underlying security. A condor spread, however, has two inner strikes in the center of the position instead of one in a butterfly spread. A condor spread contains four options with four strike prices and is effectively two spreads stacked on each other. A sophisticated options trader would establish a long condor spread when he or she expects the underlying security or index to remain in a period of low volatility. An investor who establishes a long condor spread is effectively neutral on the underlying security and does not expect a large price move. A long condor spread is established as a debit spread. Like all debit spreads, the investor's maximum loss will be equal to the net debit paid to establish the position. The investor's maximum gain for the position will be the same as for other spreads: the difference between the strike prices minus the net debit. A condor spread, like a butterfly spread and a straddle, will have two breakeven points. The breakeven point for the upper end of the position will be the higher strike price minus the debit. The breakeven point for the lower end of the position will be the lower strike price plus the debit. A long condor spread could be established as follows.

EXAMPLE   An investor establishes the following positions:

Buy 1 XYZ June 85 call at 2.

Sell 1 XYZ June 80 call at 4.

Sell 1 XYZ June 75 call at 6.

Buy 1 XYZ June 70 call at 9.

Debit	Credit
2	4
9	6

1

The investor established the position for a net debit of 1, or $100. Using the above formulas, we determine that the investor will:

- Have a maximum loss of 1, or $100.
- Have a maximum gain of $400 (5-point spread – debit).
- Have a lower breakeven of 71 (lower strike price + debit).
- Have an upper breakeven of 84 (higher strike price – debit).

The investor will realize the maximum gain on a long condor position when the underlying security is between the two short strike prices at expiration

 TAKENOTE!

An investor would establish a short condor if he or she expects a large move in the price of the underlying security. The seller of the condor, like all option sellers, has a maximum gain equal to the net credit received. The seller will realize the maximum gain if the underlying security is above or below the outer strike prices or the wings of the position at expiration.

COMBINATIONS

A combination, like a straddle, is the simultaneous purchase or sale of a call and a put on the same underlying stock with the same expiration date but with different strike prices.

Investors may establish a long combination when they feel that the stock will make a significant move in either direction. A long combination may be established as follows:

Long 1 XYZ May 70 call at 2.

Long 1 XYZ May 60 put at 1.

An investor may elect to purchase a combination instead of a straddle because the overall premium paid for the position will be less than the premium for a straddle. Although the overall risk with a long combination is less than that of the straddle, the stock will have to make a more significant move for the investor to be profitable. An investor who feels that the price of the underlying security will remain in a trading range may establish a short combination as follows:

Short 1 XYZ May 70 call at 2.

Short 1 XYZ May 60 put at 1.

An investor who sells a combination will receive less premium than an investor who sells a straddle, but will also be taking on less risk.

COLLARS

A collar is an option strategy employed by an investor who is long a stock that may be subject to downside risk or that may be range-bound for a period of time. A collar would be established by selling an upside call and by purchasing a downside put to protect the long stock position. An investor who has a profit in a stock may put on a collar to protect the gain on the stock, especially if they think that upside may be limited for a period of time. Depending on the strike prices and premiums of the options used to establish a collar, a collar could be used to generate additional income and reduce an investor's cost base while also providing some protection.

EXAMPLE

An investor bought 100 shares of XYZ at $30 per share two years ago. Since that time, the price of XYZ has increased to $43 per share. The investor is now concerned about a potential pullback in the stock. As such, the investor establishes a collar as follows:

Sell 1 XYZ May 45 call at 2

Buy 1 XYZ May 40 put at 1

By establishing this collar on XYZ, the investor has reduced their cost base (generated income) by the amount by which the premium received on the sale of the call exceeded the premium spent to purchase the put. In this example, the investor would have taken in $100 in premium income and reduced their cost base on XYZ from $30 to $29. The investor has also locked in a minimum sale price of $40 by purchasing the put.

SYNTHETIC RISK AND REWARD

Understanding the risk and reward potential of any position can substantially help investors realize their investment objectives. Certain stock and option positions have substantially similar risk and reward profiles and, as a result, have come to be known as synthetics. The following chart lists various positions and their synthetic equivalents.

Position	Synthetic
Long stock	Long call + short put
Short stock	Short call + long put
Long call	Long stock + long put
Short call	Short stock + short put
Long put	Short stock + long call
Short put	Long stock + short call

USING A T CHART TO EVALUATE OPTION POSITIONS

Many option positions can be evaluated by simply analyzing the flow of funds into or out of the investor's account. To analyze option positions, use the following T chart:

Debit	Credit

A debit in the customer's account results in an outflow of funds, whereas a credit results in an inflow of funds.

Let's analyze several option positions using the T chart. An investor buys 1 XYZ June 50 call at 5.

Debit	Credit
5	

The purchase of the call results in a net debit equal to the amount of the premium paid by the investor. To determine the investor's breakeven point, add the price that the investor would have to pay for the stock if he or he exercised the call option. This will always be equal to the call's strike price. If the investor exercised the option, the flow of funds would look as follows.

Debit	Credit
5	
50	

55

This investor would breakeven at expiration if XYZ was at 55.

Let's look at the flow of funds for an investor who buys a put. An investor purchases 1 ABC June 70 put at 4.

Debit	Credit
4	

The purchase of the put results in a net debit equal to the amount of the premium that the investor paid for the option. To determine the investor's breakeven point, enter the price that the investor would receive from exercising the put as a credit. This will always be equal to the put's strike price. Remember that owners of a put will sell the stock if they exercise the option and the sale of stock will always result in a credit into the account. If the investor exercised the option, the flow of funds will look as follows:

Debit	Credit
4	70
	66

The difference between the debit and credit will equal the investor's breakeven point.

Let's look at the flow of funds for an investor who is long stock and short a call. An investor is long 100 TRY at 50 and Short 1 TRY May 55 call at 3.

Debit	Credit
50	3
47	

The investor has paid 50 for the stock and received 3 from the sale of the call; therefore, the investor's net outlay of cash is 47, and this will be the investor's breakeven point. That is to say that the stock could fall to 47 and the investor would still break even. To determine the investor's maximum gain, enter the sales proceeds from the sale of the stock in the credit column. This will be equal to the strike price of the option if the option was exercised against the investor and the stock was called away.

Debit	Credit
50	3
	55

8

Let's look at the flow of funds for an investor who is long stock and long a put. An investor is long 100 shares of ABC at 42 and long 1 ABC November 40 put at 2.

Debit	Credit
42	
2	

44

Because the investor has purchased both the stock and the protective put, ABC must rise to 44 in order for the investor to break even. The investor's maximum loss will be realized if ABC falls and the investor has to exercise the put. To determine the maximum loss, enter the sales proceeds from the exercise of the put in the credit column.

Debit	Credit
42	40
2	

4

The investor's maximum loss will be $4 per share.

Let's look at the flow of funds for an investor who is short stock and long a call. An investor is short 100 shares of DOG at 43 and is long 1 DOG May 45 call at 3. The flow of funds will look as follows:

Debit	Credit
3	43
	40

DOG would have to fall to 40 in order for the investor to break even. The investor will realize his maximum possible loss if DOG rises and the investor has to exercise the call to close out the position. The flow of funds in that case will look as follows:

Debit	Credit
3	43
45	

5

If the investor has to repurchase DOG at 45, the investor would realize a maximum loss of $5 per share.

Let's look at the flow of funds for an investor who is short stock and short a put. An investor is short 100 shares of DOG at 43 and short 1 DOG June 40 put at 2. The flow of funds will look as follows:

Debit	Credit
	43
	2

45

DOG could rise to 45 and the investor would still break even.

If DOG falls and the stock is put to the investor at the strike price of the short put, the flow of fund will be as follows:

Debit	Credit
40	43
	2

5

If the stock is put to the investor at 40, the investor will realize the maximum profit of $5 per share.

The T chart is also effective in analyzing positions created from multiple option positions, such as straddles and spreads. Let's look at the flow of funds for a long straddle. An investor is long 1 XYZ October 70 call at 4 and long 1 XYZ October 70 put at 2.

Debit	Credit
4	
2	
6	

The investor's maximum loss is the net debit or $6 per share. Remember that a straddle has two breakevens: one for the call side and one for the put side. The investor in this case will break even at 76 on the call side and 64 on the put side. If the investor was short the straddle, the premiums would have been entered on the credit side of the chart, and that would represent the investor's maximum gain.

Spreads are created by the simultaneous purchase and sale of two options of the same type on the same underlying security that differ in strike price, expiration month, or both. Because the investor is purchasing and selling options, the T chart will have entries in both the debit and credit columns. Let's look at the flow of funds for a bull call spread.

An investor establishes the following position:

Long 1 TRY May 30 call at 2.

Short 1 TRY May 40 call at 1.

Debit	Credit
2	1
1	

The investor's maximum loss is $1 per share because that was the net debit in the account. If the investor established a bear call spread by being short this spread, the position would have resulted in a net credit in the account of $1 per share, and that would be the investor's maximum gain.

Investors can use T charts to help determine:

- Their maximum gain.
- Their maximum loss.
- Their breakeven.

Pretest

OPTION STRATEGIES

1. A bullish investor would establish which of the following?

    I. Credit put spread

    II. Long straddle

    III. Debit call spread

    IV. Short straddle

    a. I and II

    b. I and III

    c. II and III

    d. II and IV

2. You are long 10,000 shares of XYZ at 42. You are concerned about a market decline and you would like to take in some additional income. You should:

    a. Sell 10 XYZ Oct 45 puts

    b. Sell 100 XYZ Oct 45 calls

    c. Sell 100 XYZ Oct 45 puts

    d. Sell 10 XYZ Oct 45 calls

3. You bought the following:

   10 XYZ April 75 calls at 3.40

   10 XYZ April 75 puts at 4.10

   What is your maximum gain?

   a. Unlimited

   b. $67,500

   c. $7,500

   d. $82,500

4. Your customer sold 15 XYZ Aug 70 calls and bought 15 XYZ Aug 90 calls. What does your customer want to happen?

   I. The options to be exercised

   II. The options to expire

   III. The spread to widen

   IV. The spread to narrow

   a. I and IV

   b. II and IV

   c. II and III

   d. I only

5. A customer establishes the following position:

   Sold 10 ABC Oct 50 puts at 4

   Bought 10 ABC Oct 40 puts at 1

   What is the customer's maximum gain?

   a. $1,000

   b. $7,000

   c. $4,000

   d. $3,000

6. An aggressive investor sells short 1,000 shares of OnNet.com at $30 per share. To gain the maximum protection, he should:

   a. sell 10 OnNet June 30 puts.

   b. sell 10 OnNet June 30 calls.

   c. buy 10 OnNet June 30 puts.

   d. buy 10 OnNet June 30 calls.

7. Which of the following will create a diagonal spread?

   I. Short 10 XYZ Oct 50 puts

   II. Long 10 XYZ Oct 60 puts

   III. Long 10 XYZ Nov 50 puts

   IV. Long 10 XYZ Nov 40 puts

   a. I and IV

   b. II and IV

   c. I and II

   d. I and III

8. An investor who establishes which of the following may realize a gain that is unlimited?

   I. Long puts, long stock

   II. Long calls, long puts

   III. Long calls, short stock

   IV. Short calls, short puts

   a. I and IV

   b. II and IV

   c. I and II

   d. I and III

9. An investor who is long a spread will realize a loss if:

    I. The options are exercised.

    II. The spread widens.

    III. The options expire.

    IV. The spread narrows.

    a. III and IV

    b. II and IV

    c. I and II

    d. I and III

10. An investor who sells a straddle against a long stock position will:

    I. Have less risk than an investor who has written covered calls.

    II. Have received more premium income than an investor who has written covered calls.

    III. Have increased the downside risk.

    IV. Have reduced the breakeven point.

    a. III and IV

    b. I and II

    c. II, III, and IV

    d. I and III

Index, Interest Rate, and Currency Options

INTRODUCTION

The option exchanges have developed a variety of options designed to allow investors to manage risks and to gain exposure to the performance of an underlying index, interest rate environment, and currency markets. This chapter explores three of the most popular types of options: index, interest rate, and currency options, as well as options on other underlying instruments.

INDEX OPTIONS

In an effort to gauge the market's overall performance, industry participants developed indexes. Two of the most widely followed indexes are the Dow Jones Industrial Average (DJIA) and Standard and Poor's 500 (S&P 500). There are two types of indexes: broad-based indexes, such as the S&P 500 (SPX) or S&P 100 (OEX), that track a large number of stocks and narrow-based indexes, such as the semiconductor index (SOX), that track only a particular industry. The following table details some of the more popular indexes an investor can trade options on:

Broad-Based Indexes	Narrow-Based Indexes
S&P 500 (SPX)	Semiconductor Index (SOX)
S&P 100 (OEX)	Oil Index (OIX)
Dow Jones Industrials (DJX)	Pharmaceutical Index (DRG)
Nasdaq 100 (NDX)	Computer Technology (XCT)

INDEX OPTION SETTLEMENT

Investors who want to take a position in index options will purchase calls and puts just like investors in stock options. However, an index is not a security, and it cannot be physically delivered if the option is exercised. An investor cannot call the index away from someone who is short a call and cannot put an index to an investor who is short a put. As a result, the exercise of index options will be settled in cash. Option holders who elect to exercise an option will have their account credited the in-the-money amount, in cash. The amount that will be credited to their account will be the in-the-money amount at the close of the market on the day of exercise. The exercise of an index option settles between broker dealers on T + 1, and customer accounts will be credited or debited accordingly. To determine the option's premium and the amount of money to be delivered upon the exercise of index options, use 100 as a multiplier.

EXAMPLE

An investor establishes the following position:

Long 1 OEX March 550 call at $4.

The investor has purchased an S&P 100 (OEX) 550 call for $4. The contract value is 55,000, and the total premium paid by the investor is $400. The investor is bullish on the overall market and believes the market will rise and the OEX will be higher than 550 by expiration.

If at expiration the index is at 556.20, the investor's account will be credited the in-the-money amount as follows:

$$\begin{array}{r} 556.20 \\ -\ 550.00 \\ \hline 6.20 \\ \times\ 100 \\ \hline \$620.00 \end{array}$$

The investor's account will be credited $620. Because the investor paid $400 for the option, the investor's profit is $220.

EXERCISING AN INDEX OPTION

It is usually not wise to exercise an index option prior to its expiration, because the investor would lose any amount of the time value contained in the option's premium. Additionally, if the investor exercises the option at 10:00 a.m., the investor will receive the in-the-money amount as of the close of the market that day. It is quite possible for an investor to exercise the in-the-money option at 10:00 a.m. and have the option be out of the money at the close of business because the market moved against the position. In both scenarios, it is better to sell the option.

INDEX OPTION POSITIONS

An investor may establish all of the following positions using index options:

- Long calls and puts
- Short calls and puts
- Long spreads and straddles
- Short spreads and straddles
- Long and short combinations

Index options may also be used to:

- Speculate on the direction of the market.
- Protect a long portfolio by purchasing puts or selling calls.
- Protect a short portfolio by purchasing calls or selling puts.

CAPPED INDEX OPTIONS

A capped index option trades like a spread and will automatically be exercised if the underlying index closes above the capped price. Capped index options have a 30-point cap and look as follows:

Buy 1 OEX June 550 call.
Sell 1 OEX June 580 call.

If the OEX index closed above 580 at any point during the life of the option, both options will be exercised and credited the in-the-money amount. In the above example, 580 would be known as the capped price. An investor can also trade capped put options in a similar manner. A capped put option would look as follows:

Buy 1 OEX May 600 put.
Sell 1 OEX May 570 put.

In this case the capped option would automatically be exercised if the OEX closed below 570 at any point during the life of the option. With a capped put option, the lower strike price is known as the capped price.

INTEREST RATE OPTIONS

Investors can use interest rate options to speculate on the direction of interest rates or to hedge a portfolio of Treasury securities. Investors can establish a position in either price-based options or rate-based options to achieve their objectives.

PRICE-BASED OPTIONS

Price-based options are used by investors to speculate on or to hedge against a change in the price of Treasury securities. As interest rates change, the prices of Treasury securities will move in the opposite direction. Interest rates and bond prices are inversely related to each other. An investor who believes that interest rates are likely to rise would purchase price-based puts or sell price-based calls. Alternatively, an investor who believes that rates are likely to fall will purchase price-based calls or sell price-based puts. Price-based options on Treasury notes and bonds are based on the $100,000 par amount of a specific Treasury note or bond. Price-based options on Treasury bills are based on the $1,000,000 par value. Price-based options, when exercised, will result in the delivery of the specific security.

PREMIUMS ON PRICE-BASED OPTIONS: TREASURY NOTES AND BONDS
Treasury notes and bonds are priced as a percentage of par down to 32nds of 1%. Price-based options are also quoted as a percentage of par down to 32nds of 1%.

EXAMPLE   A May Treasury bond 103 call on a 7% Treasury maturing in October 2025 is quoted at 1.16. The premium is calculated as follows:

$$1.16 = 1\ 16/32\% \times \$100,000$$

$$1.5\% \times \$100,000 = \$1,500$$

The investor will pay $1,500 for the right to purchase this 7% Treasury bond maturing in October 2025 at 103.

To determine the investor's potential profit and loss on price-based options, use the same rules that were applied to equity options. The investor in our example will break even if this bond is trading at 104.16 at expiration. Price-based options settle with the delivery of the underlying security 2 business days after the option has been exercised. The buyer must pay the exercise price plus accrued interest on the underlying security.

PREMIUMS ON PRICE-BASED OPTIONS: TREASURY BILLS

Price-based options for Treasury bills are based on the $1,000,000 par value of a 13-week Treasury bill that has yet to be issued. The option's premium is quoted as an annualized percentage of the $1,000,000 par value. Because there are four 13-week quarters in a year, the premium would have to be divided by 4 to determine the amount owed or due.

EXAMPLE   A price-based Treasury bill option is quoted at 1%.

$$1\% \times \$1,000,000 = \$10,000$$

$$\$10,000/4 = \$2,500$$

 TAKENOTE!

Each basis point in the premium quote for a Treasury bill option equals $25.

Because the Treasury bill covered by the option has not yet been issued, an investor may not write a covered Treasury bill call. If a Treasury bill option is exercised, the Treasury bills will be delivered the following Thursday. Because Treasury bills are issued at a discount, the buyer does not owe accrued interest.

RATE-BASED OPTIONS

An investor may speculate on interest rates or hedge a portfolio by using rate-based options. Rate-based options are open for trading, based on the most recently issued Treasury bill, note, and bond. Because an investor cannot deliver a "rate," rate-based options settle in cash and use a contract multiplier of 100. Rate-based options have a direct correlation to a change in interest rates. An investor who believes that rates will rise would purchase rate-based calls or sell rate-based puts. An investor who believes that rates are going to fall would purchase rate-based puts or sell rate-based calls.

EXAMPLE

An investor believes that rates are going to rise and purchases 1 March 70 call at 5. The strike price of 70 equals an interest rate of 7%. The premium is 5 (5 × 100 = $500). If rates were to go to 8% by expiration, the investor would have a $500 profit.

$$\begin{array}{r} 80 \\ \underline{70} \\ 10 \end{array}$$

The 7% call option would be 10 points in the money at expiration, and the investor's account would be credited $1,000. This is found by multiplying the in-the-money amount by the contract multiplier of 100. Because the investor paid $500 for the option, the investor's profit would be $500.

	Rates Up	Rates Down	Settlement
Priced-based options	Buy puts or sell calls	Buy calls or sell puts	Underlying security is delivered
Rate-based options	Buy calls or sell puts	Buy puts or sell calls	In cash

CURRENCY MARKETS

The value of one country's currency relative to another's is constantly changing and is known as the exchange rate. Large commercial banks exchange currencies for their own accounts and for the accounts of large banks and commercial customers in the interbank market. The interbank market is a large unregulated marketplace where currencies are traded in spot and forward transactions. A spot transaction is an exchange of currencies that will settle in 2 business days. A forward transaction is an exchange of currencies that will settle on an agreed upon date that is more than 2 business days in the future. Most forward transactions will settle in either 1, 3, 6, 9, or 12 months. The exchange rate under which the currencies will be exchanged for both spot and forward transactions is agreed upon on the trade date.

SPOT RATES

The term spot rate is used by traders and investors to reference or quote the exchange rate between currencies. The spot rate can be quoted in U.S. or European terms. A U.S. quote states the number of U.S. dollars needed to purchase a unit of the relevant foreign currency. If, for example, the British pound is quoted in U.S. terms at 1.75, it takes $1.75 to purchase one British pound. The corresponding European quote would be the reciprocal of the U.S. quote. To find the European terms, use the following formula: 1/U.S. terms. In this case, 1/1.75 = .571 British pounds are required to purchase one U.S. dollar. Accordingly, the U.S. quote is the reciprocal of the European quote. If a spot rate is quoted in European terms, to find the corresponding U.S. quote use the following formula: 1/European terms.

FOREIGN CURRENCY OPTIONS

The value of one currency relative to another constantly fluctuates. The U.S. dollar is the benchmark against which the value of all other currencies is measured. During any given point, one U.S. dollar may buy more or less of another country's currency. Businesses engaged in international trade can hedge their currency risks through the use of foreign currency options. Foreign currency options may also be used by investors to speculate on the direction of a currency's value relative to the U.S. dollar.

FOREIGN CURRENCY OPTION BASICS

As the value of another country's currency rises, the value of the U.S. dollar falls. As a result, it would now take more U.S. dollars to purchase one unit of that foreign currency. Conversely, if the value of the foreign currency falls, the value of the U.S. dollar will rise, and it would now take fewer U.S. dollars to purchase one unit of the foreign currency. The value of foreign currencies is inversely related to each other. U.S. investors can only trade options on the foreign currency. No options trade domestically on the U.S. dollar. Foreign currency options trade on the Nasdaq/OMX/PHLX. The exchange sets the strike prices, expiration cycle, and the amount of the foreign currency covered under each contract. Foreign currency options that are exercised settle in the delivery of U.S. dollars. To calculate the total premium for a foreign currency option, use the following table:

Currency	Australian Dollar	British Pound	Canadian Dollar	Euro	Japanese Yen	Swiss Franc
Contract size	10,000	10,000	10,000	10,000	1,000,000	10,000
Premium quote	Cents per unit	Cents per unit	Cents per unit	Cents per unit	Hundredth of cents per unit	Cents per unit
Quote	$.01	$.01	$.01	$.01	$.0001	$.01

To calculate the total premium, multiply the quoted premium by .01. If the option is for the Japanese yen, multiply the quoted premium by .0001. Once you have determined the quoted premium, multiply it by the number of foreign currency units covered by the contract.

 TAKENOTE!

You will not be required to remember the amount of the foreign currency covered under the contract. If you receive a question relating to foreign currency, the question will contain the amount of the foreign currency covered under the contract.

BUYING FOREIGN CURRENCY CALLS AND PUTS

Businesses and investors trade foreign currency options for very different reasons. A business will trade foreign currency options to manage its foreign currency risk. An importer will purchase calls on the foreign currency of the country where it purchases products to reduce the risk of that country's currency rising in value in relation to the U.S. dollar. If the country's currency becomes stronger, it will take more U.S. dollars to purchase the same amount of the foreign currency. As a result, the cost to the importer will rise. Alternatively, in the case of an exporter, a fall in the value of a foreign currency will make its products more expensive to the foreign customer and will make its products less attractive. As a result, the exporter, to manage their foreign currency risk, will purchase puts on the foreign currency. An investor who exercises a foreign currency put or call option will have their account credited the in-the-money amount. Investors in foreign currency options can establish all the same positions that an investor in stock or index options can, such as spreads, straddles, combinations, covered calls, and protective puts.

 TESTTIP!

Remember the mnemonic EPIC: exporters buy puts; importers buy calls.

An investor in foreign currency options would take the following positions given the following circumstances.

An investor would buy calls or sells puts if:

- There is good economic news from that country.
- The stock market in that country rises.
- There is a large discovery of oil or gold in that country.
- Government instability subsides.

An investor would buy puts and sell calls if:

- There is bad economic news from that country.
- The stock market in that country falls.
- There is an increase in political instability.

The following rules have been set for foreign currency options expiration and exercise:

- Foreign currency options trade on the OMX/PHLX from 9:30 a.m. to 4:00 p.m. EST.
- Options expire at 11:59 p.m. EST the third Friday and must be exercised by 5:30 p.m. EST.
- Position limits are 600,000 contracts on the same side of the market.

MARKET VOLATILITY OPTIONS (VIX)

The rate of change in prices is known as volatility. Active traders in many cases need both volatility in prices and changes in volatility of prices to realize profits. Investors can also speculate on market volatility by trading VIX options. VIX options measure the market volatility of the S&P 500 (SPX) based on the spread between the bid and ask of S&P 500 index options. The VIX calculation uses the spread from the two closest option expiration cycles with at least 8 days remaining to expiration to calculate a 30-day volatility for the index. VIX options trade from 8:30 a.m. to 3:15 p.m. CST in 2-1/2 point intervals and differ from other options in several ways. VIX options:

- Are European-style.
- Expire 30 days prior to the third Friday of the following month.
- Settle under the symbol VRO.

FLEX OPTIONS

Large and sophisticated investors often need to set up trades based on their specific needs. For these investors, the terms and conditions of standardized options often do not meet their requirements. Flex options allow investors to set:

- The expiration.
- The strike price.
- The expiration style (American or European).
- The value of the contract.

The expiration for flex options can be up to 3 years. However, a flex option may not expire on any day that is on or within 2 business days of a non-flex-option expiration date. A trader must present the specifics of the desired flex option contract in the trading crowd to receive a market or quote for the flex option. The exchanges may set minimum values for flex options contracts, and there is no active secondary market for the flex option after the position has been established. Flex options can trade on the following instruments:

- Equities
- Indexes
- Currencies

The exercise of the flex option does not result in the delivery of the underlying security.

WEEKLY OPTIONS

The CBOE has introduced weekly options to provide investors with the ability to speculate on the direction of a stock or index based on the release of pending news, such as an earnings release or an announcement from the Federal Reserve Board relating to an interest rate decision. Weekly options will also allow investors who are long or short to hedge their positions for only the period of time that includes the pending news release. As such, the investor will be able to buy the hedge at a much lower premium due to the extremely short time frame of the option. Weekly options are listed on Thursday and expire the following Friday. New weekly options are listed each week; however, no new weekly options are listed that would expire during the expiration week for standard options (the third Friday of each month).

BINARY OPTIONS

Binary options are a way to speculate on the price of an underlying index based on your opinion of where a market will be in a certain period of time. Binary options are contracts that, at expiration, pay out a predetermined fixed amount or nothing at all. The payout amount for CBOE binary options is $100 per contract.

Binary options are based on an underlying security, have various strike prices, and various expirations. CBOE lists both call and put binary options.

If, at expiration, the price of the underlying security closes at or above the selected strike price, the buyer of a binary call option receives $100 per contract. If the underlying security closes at a price that is below the strike price on the expiration date, the buyer receives nothing.

In the case of binary put options, the put buyer receives $100 per contract if the underlying security closes below the strike price at expiration, and nothing if the underlying security closes at or above the strike price at expiration. As with traditional options, a binary option position may be liquidated (bought or sold to close) prior to expiration. The price of a binary option usually reflects the perceived probability that the underlying security price will reach or exceed (for binary call options) or fail to reach or exceed (for binary put options) the selected strike price at expiration. The cost of CBOE binary options will normally be quoted at a price between zero and $1 (which equates to $1 to $100 per contract). Buyers of binary options pay for the contract at the time of purchase.

MINI OPTIONS

The options exchanges have begun offering option contracts that allow an investor to speculate or to hedge a position in a high-priced security that is less than 100 shares. With many stocks trading well into the triple digits, individual investors often can only afford to purchase a small number of shares (also known as an odd lot). These investors who wish to hedge a small position would not be able to effectively do so with a standard option contract covering 100 shares. Mini options cover 10 shares of the underlying security.

To determine the total premium an investor would pay or receive, you must multiply the premium by the 10 shares covered under the contract rather than 100 shares for a standard option contract. Mini stock options are American style exercise and the exercise of mini stock options will result in the delivery of the underlying shares. Options also trade on the mini S&P 500. The mini S&P 500 contract has a value equal to 1/10 of the value of the S&P 500 contract. For example, if the S&P 500 was trading at 1,950 the mini contract would be trading at 195. Options on the mini S&P use a multiplier of 100. Options on the mini S&P are European exercise and can only be exercised at expiration. The exercise of options on the mini S&P result in the delivery of cash.

Pretest

INDEX, INTEREST RATE, AND CURRENCY OPTIONS

1. An investor who is short 1 U.S. T-bond 103 call receives an exercise notice. The investor will receive which of the following?

    I. $10,300

    II. $103,000

    III. Accrued interest

    IV. A full semiannual interest payment

    a. I and IV

    b. II and IV

    c. II and III

    d. I and III

2. You think that bond prices are going to decline, and you want to profit from the move. You would most likely buy which of the following?

    I. Rate-based puts

    II. Rate-based calls

    III. Price-based puts

    IV. Price-based calls

    a. II and III

    b. I and IV

    c. I and III

    d. III and IV

3. A U.S. importer is buying $10,000,000 worth of goods from a Japanese manufacturer. The payment will be made 6 months from now in Japanese Yen. As a hedge, the U.S. importer would do which of the following?

   a. Buy calls on the U.S. dollar

   b. Buy puts on the U.S. dollar

   c. Buy calls on the Japanese Yen

   d. Buy puts on the Japanese Yen

4. Capped index options automatically exercise if they go how far in the money?

   a. 60 points

   b. 30 points

   c. 50 points

   d. 100 points

5. A fixed-income investor may not:

   a. Write a price-based covered call.

   b. Write a rate-based covered call.

   c. Write a price-based put spread.

   d. Write a rate-based put spread.

6. A May 105 Treasury Bond call is quoted at 1.08. The investor thinks that interest rates will fall. How much would the option investor pay to purchase the call?

   a. $125

   b. $1,250

   c. $108

   d. $1,080

7. As it relates to foreign currency options, which of the following are NOT true?

    I. The U.S. dollar is the base currency.

    II. The position limit is 250,000 contracts.

    III. All premiums are quoted in tenths of a cent.

    IV. Options are available in American exercise only.

    a. I and III

    b. II and IV

    c. I and II

    d. II, III, and IV

8. When calculating the premium for a foreign currency option, which of the following is NOT moved two places to the left?

    a. British pound

    b. Euro

    c. Canadian dollar

    d. Japanese yen

9. Currency options expire:

    a. On the third Friday.

    b. On the Tuesday following the third Friday.

    c. On the Saturday following the third Friday.

    d. On the Tuesday preceding the third Wednesday.

10. Which of the following settle in cash?

    I. A rate-based call

    II. An index option

    III. A foreign currency option

    IV. A price-based put

    a. III and IV

    b. I and II

    c. I, II, and III

    d. I, II, III, and IV

The Options Marketplace

INTRODUCTION

Listed options trade on exchanges in a manner that is similar to the trading in listed stocks. The exchanges maintain orderly markets for listed options and provide investors with a marketplace to buy and sell options. Because options are derivative securities and there are different types, classes, and series of options, the options market has some unique trading features.

THE OPTION CLEARING CORPORATION

The Option Clearing Corporation (OCC) was created and is owned by the exchanges that trade options. It is regulated by the SEC. The OCC issues all standardized options and guarantees their performance. The OCC does not guarantee a customer against a loss; it only guarantees the option's performance. The OCC guarantees that if an investor who is short an option is unable to perform his or her obligation under the contract, the investor who is exercising the contract will still be able to do so without any delay. Without this performance guarantee, the trading of standardized options would be impossible. The OCC issues option contracts the day after the trade date, and all standardized options will settle on the next business day, or $T + 1$. When an investor closes out a position through either a closing purchase or sale, the OCC will eliminate the closing investor's obligations or rights from its books. All standardized options of the same series are interchangeable (fungible). For example, all XYZ April 50 calls are the same. In order to meet the prospectus requirements of the Securities Act of 1933, the OCC publishes a disclosure document known as the Characteristics and Risks of Standardized Options. All option investors must be given this document prior to or at the time their account is approved for option trading.

THE OPTIONS MARKETS

Standardized options trade on exchanges through a dual-auction process similar to that for listed stocks. All standardized options are known as listed options. However, large institutions may trade specialized options over the counter (OTC). The terms and conditions of the contract may be negotiated with the OTC option dealer. Listed options trade on the following exchanges:

- CBOE
- NYSE/AMEX
- Nasdaq/OMX/PHLX
- PSE

Although the NYSE is the premier exchange for listed stocks, the Chicago Board Options Exchange is the premier exchange for listed options. The directors of the exchanges that trade options determine which options to trade based on public interest in the underlying security. They also set the expiration cycles and strike prices for the options that trade on their floors. The exchanges generally set the strike prices for most stocks and exchange-traded funds (ETFs) in $1 intervals; options for higher-priced stocks can be set in $5 or $10 intervals.

If any option fails to meet the exchange's listing requirements, no new option series for that underlying security will be opened for trading by the exchange unless the option receives an exception from the exchange. If no exception is received, existing option series for the underlying security will continue to trade until the last series of options expires.

 **TAKENOTE!**

A customer must be notified prior to executing a transaction in an existing series of options that will be delisted.

The option exchanges have also set maximum limits on the spread between the bid and ask for option contracts that trade on their floors. The maximum spread depends on the price of the option contract and is currently set as follows:

- Bid price is less than $2: Maximum spread is 25 cents.
- Bid price is greater or equal to $2 but less than $5: Maximum spread is 40 cents.
- Bid price is greater or equal to $5 but less than $10: Maximum spread is 50 cents.
- Bid price is greater or equal to $10 but less than $20: Maximum spread is 80 cents.
- Bid price is greater than $20: Maximum spread is $1.

THE CHICAGO BOARD OPTIONS EXCHANGE

The CBOE functions in many ways exactly like other exchanges, except it has one major difference. The CBOE does not use a specialist system like the one used on all other exchanges. The specialist system requires that specialist members maintain a fair and orderly market in the securities in which they specialize and that they buy and sell for their own accounts. However, on the CBOE the duty of maintaining a fair and orderly market is given to an exchange employee known as an order book official. The personnel trading on the options floors are:

- An order book official/specialist.
- A market maker/registered option trader/local.
- A spread broker.
- A commission house broker.
- A two-dollar broker.

ORDER BOOK OFFICIAL/BOARD BROKER

Order book officials on the CBOE are employees of the exchange who maintain a fair and orderly market for the options they have been assigned. Order book officials also maintain a book of limit and stop orders left with them and will execute them when the order's conditions are met. Order book officials may only accept orders left with them by members for the accounts of public customers. Member firms may not leave orders for the official to execute for the member's own account. Order book officials may not trade for their own accounts or be associated with a member firm. A board broker or a floor par official is an exchange member who has been appointed to maintain a fair and orderly market in options.

SPECIALIST

Specialists are members of any other option exchange who are required to maintain a fair and orderly market for the options in which they specialize. Specialists are required to buy and sell from their own accounts in the absence of public orders and must execute stop and limit orders left with them. Specialists, unlike order book officials, are members of the exchange, not employees of the exchange, and, unlike order book officials, are required to trade for their own accounts.

OPTIONS MARKET MAKERS

Options market makers are individual members of the exchange who are required to maintain a two-sided market in the options they trade. A two-sided market consists of both a bid and an offer. An options market maker must display a two-sided market at all times. An options market maker may also be called a registered options trader or a local. These members trade for their own profit and loss. Options market makers must meet the financial requirements of the exchange and qualify through examination to be members of the exchange. Market makers are also required to register in the options they trade and may not be affiliates with the option's board broker in the options they trade. The main function of the market maker in the marketplace is to improve liquidity and to narrow option spreads.

COMMISSION HOUSE BROKER

A commission house broker is an employee of a member organization and will execute orders for the member's customers and for the member's own account.

TWO-DOLLAR BROKER

Two-dollar brokers are independent members who execute orders for commission house brokers when they are too busy managing other orders. Floor brokers may not accept orders directly from public customers unless they are registered and approved by the exchange to do so.

SPREAD BROKER

A spread broker is an independent member who specializes in executing multiple option orders, such as spreads and straddles, for a fee.

OPENING AND CLOSING OPTION PRICES

Options begin trading as soon as an opening price for the underlying security may be determined. Options are opened for trading through a rotation that accepts orders and quotes for the series of calls that expire the soonest and have the lowest strike price. The rotation continues through all the near-term series of call options and continues to the call options that expire further out. Once all of the calls are open, the rotation continues with the puts, starting with the puts with the highest strike price and the nearest expiration. The rotation in the puts continues through puts with lower strike prices and then to further out expirations.

Listed options also close on a rotation as soon as a closing price can be determined for the underlying security. A rotation can also be imposed during fast market conditions if the specialist or the order book official determines that the market is not operating in an orderly fashion. If a stock is halted, all option trading on that stock is also halted until the stock reopens.

FAST MARKETS AND TRADING HALTS

A sudden influx of orders as a result of news can result in fast market conditions in the option markets. If two floor officials agree that the conditions are such that the integrity of the market is compromised as a result of the fast market conditions, the floor officials can:

- Institute a trading rotation.
- Assign trading of options to another board broker.
- Allow board broker clerks to execute orders.
- Temporarily suspend the firm quote rule and AutoEx.
- Take other actions that may be required.

If the integrity of the markets cannot be restored after taking these actions, trading may be halted in the options if two floor officials agree. Trading can be halted by the floor officials for up to two business days if the underlying stock is halted, has a delayed opening, or if other unusual circumstances exist. Only the board of directors at the CBOE can suspend the trading of options if the trading in the option has been halted for two days or if the underlying security has been suspended on its principal exchange or other unusual circumstances exist. The exchange during unusual market conditions may also suspend the use of stop and limit orders to help restore the market's integrity.

CLEARLY ERRONEOUS REPORTS

If a registered representative reports the execution of a trade to a customer and that report is clearly an error, then that report is not binding on the agent or the firm. The customer must accept the trade as it actually occurred, not as it was erroneously reported, so long as the transaction was in line with the terms of the order.

EXECUTION ERRORS

If a transaction is executed away from a customer's limit price or is executed for too many contracts, the customer in not obligated to accept the transaction. A registered representative who is informed of an execution error should immediately inform the principal of the error. If the firm has executed an order at the wrong price, size, or side of the market or in the wrong contract, the trade should promptly be moved into the firm's error account and offset as soon as possible. If the error involved a customer order, the order as it was executed will be recorded into the error account and subsequently posted to the customer's account in line with the customer's instructions. This action is commonly known as a cancel and rebill. A cancel and rebill is an appropriate way to correct a trade executed in error but this action can be a red flag for suspicious activities at the firm. Execution errors for too many contracts or away from a customer's limit price are examples of trades that will be moved to the error account. The traders or representatives who move trades to the error account must fully document the error for review by the principal. If a customer makes an error entering the terms of an order over an online trading platform, the customer is obligated to accept the execution in line with the terms entered, not as intended. The customer in this case should be advised to execute an order to reverse the trade over the online trading portal.

ORDER EXECUTION

Most customer orders, which are market orders or executable limit orders, will be routed electronically to the trading post for automatic execution. The electronic system bypasses the firm's commission house broker, the order is executed automatically, and an execution report is sent back to the brokerage firm. More complex orders will be handled by the firm's commission house broker. A member firm may not execute an order for a listed option off the floor of the exchange unless it has tried to execute the order on the floor and a better price is available in another trading venue.

TYPES OF ORDERS

Investors can enter various types of orders to buy or sell options. Some orders guarantee that the investor's order will be executed immediately. Other types of orders may state a specific price or condition under which the investor wants the order to be executed. All orders are considered "day" orders unless otherwise specified. All day orders will be canceled at the end of the trading day if they are not executed. An investor may also specify that the order remain active until canceled. This type of order is known as *good 'til cancel* or *GTC*.

MARKET ORDERS

A market order will guarantee that the investor's order is executed as soon as the order is presented to the market. A market order to either buy or sell guarantees the execution but not the price at which the order will be executed. When a market order is presented for execution, the market for the option may be very different from the market that was displayed when the order was entered. As a result, the investor does not know the exact price that the order will be executed at.

BUY LIMIT ORDERS

A buy limit order sets the maximum price that the investor will pay for the option. The order may never be executed at a price higher than the investor's limit price. Although a buy limit order guarantees that the investor will not pay over a certain price, it does not guarantee that the order will be executed. If the option continues to trade higher away from the investor's limit price, the investor will not purchase the option and may miss a chance to realize a profit.

SELL LIMIT ORDERS

A sell limit order sets the minimum price that the investor will accept for the option. The order may never be executed at a price lower than the investor's limit price. Although a sell limit order guarantees that the investor will not receive less than a certain price, it does not guarantee that the order will be executed. If the option continues to trade lower away from the investor's limit price, the investor will not sell the option and may miss a chance to realize a profit or may realize a loss as a result.

 FOCUSPOINT

It's important to remember that even if an investor sees options trading at the limit price, it does not mean that the order was executed, because there could have been orders ahead of the investor's order at that limit price.

STOP ORDERS/STOP LOSS ORDERS

A stop order or stop loss order can be used by investors to limit or guard against a loss or to protect a profit. A stop order will be placed away from the market in case the option starts to move against the investor. A stop order is not a "live" order; it has to be elected. A stop order is elected and becomes a live order when the option trades at or through the stop price. The stop price is also known as the trigger price. Once the option has traded at or through the stop price, the order becomes a market order to either buy or sell the option, depending on the type of order that was placed.

BUY STOP ORDERS

A buy stop order is placed above the market and is used to protect against a loss or to protect a profit on a short sale of an option. A buy stop order could also be used by a technical analyst to get long an option.

SELL STOP ORDERS

A sell stop order is placed below the market and is used to protect against a loss or to protect a profit on the purchase of an option. A sell stop order could also be used by a technical analyst to get short an option.

STOP LIMIT ORDERS

Investors would enter a stop limit order for the same reasons they would enter a stop order. The only difference is that once the order has been elected, the order becomes a limit order instead of a market order. The same risks that apply to traditional limit orders apply to stop limit orders. If the option continues to trade away from the investor's limit, the investor could give back all of the profits or suffer large losses.

OTHER TYPES OF ORDERS

Investors may enter into several other types of orders:

- All or none (AON).
- Immediate or cancel (IOC).
- Fill or kill (FOK).
- Not held (NH).
- Market on open/market on close.

ALL OR NONE (AON) ORDERS

AON orders may be entered as day orders or GTC. All or none orders, as the name implies, indicate that the investor wants to buy or sell all of the options or none of them. AON orders are not displayed in the market because of the required special handling, and the investor will not accept a partial execution.

IMMEDIATE OR CANCEL (IOC) ORDERS

With IOC orders, investors want to buy or sell whatever contracts they can immediately and whatever orders are not filled are canceled.

FILL OR KILL (FOK) ORDERS

With FOK orders, the investor wants the entire order executed immediately or the entire order canceled.

NOT HELD (NH) ORDERS

With NH orders, the investor gives discretion to the floor broker as to the time and price of execution. All retail NH orders given to a representative are considered day orders unless the order is received in writing from the customer and entered as GTC.

SPREAD ORDERS

With spread orders, orders to establish or liquidate spreads are entered on one order ticket and are executed in a single transaction on the floor of the exchange. Larger spread orders may be handled by floor brokers who specialize in spread orders and are known as spread brokers. Orders for spreads can be entered as market orders or as limit orders. Spread limit orders will be entered as orders stating the net debit or credit to be paid or received. A spread order will identify the number of options to be bought and sold as follows:

Buy 10 TRY June 70 calls.

Sell 10 TRY June 80 calls.

If this was a limit order, the price of both options would be listed and the difference in premiums would be the debit the investor would be willing to pay for the spread.

PRIORITY OF OPTION ORDERS

The acceptance of bids and offers for exchange-listed options are filled on a first come, first serve basis, with the highest bid or lowest offer being filled first. Customer orders that are entered at the same price as a member's order will be given priority over the member's order. If two member orders are competing at the same price, priority will be given to the member order that was entered first. Spread orders are given priority over single option orders.

TRADE REPORTING

When a transaction takes place on the floor of the exchange, the member firm on the sell side of the transaction must report the trade to the clerk to be displayed on the tape. Members that execute orders transmitted to the floor of the exchange must then report the execution to the originating party. All orders sent to the floor must be sent in writing on an exchange-approved form. Orders transmitted by member firms through wire or telephone must be sent through exchanged-approved communication facilities. Orders received through these facilities will, in most cases, be written on exchange-approved order tickets by the order clerks who receive the order. At the end of each trading day, clearing members are required to report all option trades to the exchange. These reports will include orders executed for the clearing member's own account as well as orders executed for the accounts of the clearing member's customers (introducing broker dealers). The exchange compares all trades submitted by all clearing members at the end of the day and will notify members of any unmatched trades. Members are required to reconcile all open unmatched trades contained in the report by 9:30 a.m. EST on T + 1 and to notify the exchange of the resolution by that time. All matched trades are reported by the exchange to the OCC on a daily basis. The OCC, in turn, sends a daily report to each clearing member detailing the previous day's matched trades, net premiums owed or due to the OCC, and any assignment notices.

OPTION ORDER TICKETS

Prior to transmitting a customer's option order, the representative must fill out the appropriate order ticket and present it to the trading department or wire room for execution. All order tickets will include:

- Buy or sell.
- The name of the underlying security.
- Number of contracts.
- Type of option.
- Expiration date.
- Exercise price.
- An indication if the transaction is opening or closing the contracts.
- If an opening sale, a notation regarding covered or uncovered is required.
- Account name and number.
- Account type (i.e., cash or margin).
- Price and time limits, if any.
- Solicited or unsolicited.
- Discretionary authority exercised or discretionary authority not exercised, if applicable.
- Time stamp when entered, executed, changed, or canceled.

EXPIRATION AND EXERCISE

The OCC has set the following rules for the expiration and exercise of stock and narrow-based index options:

- Options cease trading at 4:00 p.m. EST (3:00 p.m. CST) on the third Friday of each month prior to expiration.
- Option holders who wish to exercise their options must do so by 5:30 p.m. EST (4:30 p.m. CST), the third Friday prior to expiration.

- All options expire at 11:59 p.m. EST (10:59 p.m. CST) on the third Friday of each month.
- All options held by public customers will automatically be exercised if they are 1 cent in the money.
- All options held by broker dealers will automatically be exercised if they are 1 cent in the money.

The OCC has set the following rules for the expiration and exercise of broad-based options:

- Options cease trading at 4:15 p.m. EST (3:15 p.m. CST) on the third Friday prior to expiration.
- Option holders who wish to exercise their options must do so by 5:30 p.m. EST (4:30 p.m. CST) the third Friday prior to expiration.
- All options expire at 11:59 p.m. EST (10:59 p.m. CST) on the third Friday of each month.

AMERICAN VS. EUROPEAN EXERCISE

There are two styles of options that trade in the United States: American and European. An American-style option may be exercised at any time by the holder during the life of the contract. A European-style option may only be exercised by the holder at expiration.

If an investor who is long an option decides to exercise the option, the OCC will randomly assign the exercise notice to a broker dealer who is short that option. The broker dealer must then assign the exercise notice to a customer who is short that option. The broker dealer may use any fair method for randomly assigning exercise notices.

POSITION AND EXERCISE LIMITS

Certain market participants who directly or indirectly exercise investment discretion over one or more accounts are required to register as large traders with the SEC. These large traders will be assigned a large trader ID (LTID). The large trader is required to provide its LTID to each broker dealer that executes orders for the large trader. The executing broker dealer is required to record all transactions executed for the large trader and the LTID and time must be noted on each order. The large trader must file form 13H with the SEC within 45 days of the end of each calendar year. A large trader is defined as an entity that:

> Executes a trade or trades in an NMS security of two million shares or greater or with a value of $20 million or greater on a single day; or

> Executes a trade or trades in an NMS security of 20 million shares or greater or with a value of $200 million or greater in a calendar quarter; or

> Executes a trade or trades in options which meet the daily or quarterly limits above based on the value or number of the underlying shares covered by the option contracts.

In order to prevent large investors from manipulating the price of a stock or the value of an index, the exchanges have set maximum limits for the size of a position that may be established on the same side of the market. The current maximum limit is 250,000 contracts on the same side of the market. A position limit for any underlying security is also the exercise limit that an investor or group of investors acting in concert may exercise in any 5 consecutive business days. The limits are assigned based on the underlying security's volume and number of outstanding shares. The position limits are reviewed every 6 months, and forward stock splits and stock dividends will temporarily increase the position and the exercise limits.

The bullish side of the market is:

- Long calls and short puts.

The bearish side of the market is:

- Long puts and short calls.

EXAMPLE If an investor is long 40,000 calls, the maximum number of puts the investor could sell is 35,000, if the maximum position limit was 75,000 contracts.

STOCK SPLITS AND STOCK DIVIDENDS

Whenever an underlying security declares a stock split or a substantial stock dividend, the terms of the option contract must be adjusted. The exam will focus on forward stock splits. When a company declares a forward stock split, such as a 2 for 1 or 3 for 1, the number of contracts will increase, and the option's strike price will be adjusted down. Each contract will still be for 100 shares, and the investor's aggregate exercise price will always remain the same. To determine the new number of contracts and the new strike price for a class of options after an even forward stock split, multiply the number of contracts by the split and multiply the strike price by the reciprocal of the split.

EXAMPLE

XYZ declares a 2 for 1 stock split. An investor holding 5 XYZ June 60 calls would now own 10 XYZ June 30 calls:

- 2/1 × 5 contracts = 10 contracts.
- ½ × $60 strike price = $30 strike price.
- The aggregate exercise price (value) both before and after the split is $3,000.

If the split that was declared by the company is not an even split, the number of shares covered by the contract will increase, and the strike price will be adjusted down. If a contract is for more than 100 shares an * (asterisk) will appear next to the quote.

EXAMPLE

Type of Split	Old Contract	New Contract
2:1	1 XYZ Oct 70 call	2 XYZ Oct 35 calls
4:1	5 ABC April 60 puts	20 ABC April 15 puts
3:2	1 XYZ April 60 call	1 (150 sh) April 40 call

Options are not adjusted for cash dividends but are adjusted for stock dividends.

EXAMPLE

If an investor owns 1 XYZ May 40 call and XYZ declares a 25% stock dividend, the investor will now own 1 XYZ (125) May 32 call. The adjusted or new number of shares covered by the contract is found by multiplying the number of shares in the contract by the stock dividend percent and adding the additional shares to the contract shares. In this case, 100 shares × 25% = 25 shares, 100 + 25 = 125 shares. The adjusted or new exercise price is found as follows:

aggregate exercise price

adjusted number of shares

4,000

125

4,000/125 = 32

The number of shares covered by the contract will increase and the strike price will be adjusted down. The number of shares is rounded down to the next whole share if required.

Pretest

THE OPTIONS MARKETPLACE

1. Which of the following is true of the OCC?

   a. It is wholly owned by the exchanges.

   b. It is wholly owned by the NYSE and FINRA.

   c. It is the self-regulatory body for the option industry.

   d. It is a division of the SEC.

2. Which of the following are true of order book officials?

   I. They are employees of the exchange.

   II. They are required to provide liquidity to the market by acting as a principal.

   III. They execute orders for members.

   IV. They supervise the opening rotations.

   a. I and III

   b. II and IV

   c. I, III, and IV

   d. I, II, III, and IV

3. An investor who exercises his long calls on Friday at 3:42 p.m. EST will receive the underlying shares on:

   a. Friday.

   b. Monday.

   c. Tuesday.

   d. Wednesday.

4. If the underlying stock trades ex-dividend on Monday, October 5th, a put writer who has been exercised on Friday, October 2:

   a. Would pay the dividend to the put holder.

   b. Would be entitled to receive the dividend.

   c. Would not be entitled to receive the dividend.

   d. Would have to send the put holder a due bill to collect the dividend.

5. An option holder who wants to exercise his options just prior to expiration must send an exercise notice by:

   a. 3:30 p.m. CST.

   b. 4:30 p.m. EST.

   c. 5:00 p.m. EST.

   d. 4:30 p.m. CST.

6. If you own a call option and the underlying stock splits 2 for 1, what is the result?

   I. The option increases to two times as many shares.

   II. The exercise price decreases.

   III. The exercise price increases.

   IV. The number of contracts increases.

   a. II and III

   b. II and IV

   c. I and II

   d. I and III

7. Which of the following is true of OCC assignments of an exercise notice to a member firm?

   a. The most frequent trader will be assigned.

   b. Assignments will be done on a random basis only.

   c. The exercise will be assigned to whoever has the largest short position.

   d. Assignments will be done on a FIFO basis only.

8. Which of the following are NOT true of the option market and the OCC?

   I. The OCC assigns exercise notices directly to a customer who is short the option.

   II. An investor who closes out a short option contract has his obligations eliminated by the OCC.

   III. The OCC is the SRO for the options markets.

   IV. The OCC is owned by the option exchanges.

   a. I and III

   b. II and IV

   c. I and IV

   d. II and III

9. Which of the following are true of the option markets?

   I. Options expire at 10:59 p.m. CST on the third Friday.

   II. The position limit for foreign currency options is 150,000 contracts.

   III. Equity options that are exercised will result in the delivery of the stock the next business day.

   IV. Equity options cease trading at 4:00 p.m. EST the day of expiration.

   a. I and III

   b. II and IV

   c. I and IV

   d. I, II, III, and IV

10. Which of the following are FALSE with regard to option trading rotations?

    I. The OCC may institute a trading rotation for a new option contract on the day it first trades.

    II. Put options with the lowest strike price are the first puts quoted in any rotation.

    III. Floor officials can institute a trading rotation during fast markets.

    IV. All option exchanges use opening and closing option rotations.

    a. I and II

    b. II and IV

    c. I and IV

    d. II and III

Option Taxation and Margin Requirements

INTRODUCTION

Investors who buy and sell options need to understand how option transactions will impact their tax liability. Buying and selling options creates a taxable event and using options to hedge an underlying position can impact the investment's holding period and cost base. This chapter examines how gains and losses related to options are taxed and the margin requirements for options.

TAXATION OF OPTIONS

An investor who purchases a call or put that expires worthless will have a short-term capital loss. An investor who purchases long-term LEAPS (long-term equity anticipation securities), which have a term of up to 39 months that eventually expire, will have a long-term capital loss. The writer of both LEAPS and traditional options that expire worthless will have a short-term capital gain.

EXAMPLE

An investor buys 10 FGH May 40 calls at 1. If at expiration, FGH is at 37 and the investor allows the calls to expire, the investor will have a $1,000 loss. Alternatively, if the investor who sold the 10 FGH May 40 calls at 1 allows the calls to expire, the investor will have a $1,000 capital gain.

CLOSING AN OPTION POSITION

Executing an order to close an option position will result in a capital gain or capital loss if the closing price differs from the opening price.

| EXAMPLE | An investor buys 5 TRY August 40 calls at 4. If TRY increases in price to 47 and the investor sells the calls at 9, the investor will have a $2,500 capital gain. The investor paid 4 for the calls and sold them at 9, resulting in a $5 per share profit on 500 shares. Alternatively, if TRY fell to 41 and the investor closes out the position by selling the calls at 1, the investor would have a $1,500 capital loss. The investor would have lost $3 per share on 500 shares. |

| EXAMPLE | An investor who sells 2 ABC July 60 puts at 7 and covers the position with a closing purchase by buying back the puts at 2 will have a $1,000 capital gain. The investor made $5 per share on 200 shares. Alternatively, if ABC fell in price and the investor covered the short puts with a closing purchase by buying back the puts at 11, the investor would have an $800 loss. The investor lost $4 per share on 200 shares. |

EXERCISING A CALL

If an investor exercises a call option, the option's premium is added to the investor's cost base for the stock to determine any capital gain or capital loss. For tax purposes, the holding period for the stock begins when the call is exercised. If an investor wrote a call, the call option's premium must be added to the option's strike price to determine the investor's proceeds on the sale of the stock if the stock is called away.

| EXAMPLE | An investor buys 1 JKL September 60 call at 3 on Tuesday July 7. If on Monday, August 2, JKL is trading at 68 and the investor exercises the call, the investor's holding period would begin on August 2 not on July 7, when the investor purchased the call. The investor's cost base for JKL after exercising the call is 63, which is the call's strike price plus the premium. |

| EXAMPLE | An investor who sells 1 RTG May 40 call at 5 and has the stock called away will have an effective sale price for RTG of $45. Investors who sell calls and have the stock called away must add the call option's premium to the strike price to determine the sale proceeds for tax purposes. |

EXERCISING A PUT

An investor who exercises a put must subtract the put's premium from the option's strike price to determine the proceeds from the sale. A put writer who is exercising a put must subtract the premium from the strike price to determine the cost base for the stock. An investor who is short a put and who is assigned the stock will subtract the premium received from the strike price to determine the cost base for tax purposes.

EXAMPLE   An investor purchases 1 CVB October 70 put at 3. If CVB falls to 60 and the investor purchases the stock and exercises the put, the investor will have a $700 capital gain. The investor purchased the stock at 60 and subtracts the premium paid for the put from the strike price to determine the sale proceeds. In this case 70 − 3 = 67.

EXAMPLE   An investor who sells 1 KLM November 80 put at 9 and who is assigned the stock will have a cost base for the stock of 71.

PROTECTIVE PUTS

An investor who has purchased a protective put on a stock held less than 12 months will cap the holding period for that stock at 12 months and will have a short-term gain or loss on the sale of the stock. If the stock was held for more than 12 months before purchasing the put, any gain or loss will be long-term. Married puts purchased on the same day as the stock will not automatically create a short-term gain or loss for the stock so long as the puts are identified as a hedge or as married puts when the order is executed. If the put expires, the put's premium is added to the stock's cost base.

COVERED CALLS

An investor who sells out of the money calls will not change the holding period for the stock if the calls expire. An investor who sells deep in-the-money calls on a stock held less than 12 month will have a short-term gain or loss.

OPTION CONTRACT MARGIN REQUIREMENTS

Investors who purchase option contracts must meet the margin requirements for the position promptly. The investor's margin requirement for the position varies with the type of option position established by the investor.

Traditional options have no loan value, and investors are required to deposit 100% of the option's premium under Regulation T on T + 3, or two business days after settlement. Because option contracts settle the next business day, most brokerage firms require that the investor deposit the required funds by T + 1. An investor may purchases LEAPS with an expiration exceeding nine months by depositing 75% of the option's premium in a margin account.

MARGIN REQUIREMENTS WHEN EXERCISING A CALL

When an investor exercises a call, the underlying stock transaction will settle regular way on T + 2. For settlement and payment dates, the exercise date is considered the trade date. If an investor exercises a call in a cash account, the investor must deposit the entire exercise value of the contract by the payment date. If an investor exercises a call option in a margin account, the required Regulation T deposit must be met by the payment date. An exception to these deposit requirements would be if an investor exercises a call and sells the stock on the same day. This would result in a cashless exercise and would not require additional funds to be deposited.

MARGIN REQUIREMENTS WHEN EXERCISING A PUT

When an investor exercises a put, the underlying stock transaction will settle regular way on T + 2. If an investor exercises a put in a cash account, the investor must be long the stock in the account or must deposit the stock by the settlement date. If an investor is not long the underlying stock and exercises a put option in a margin account, the required Regulation T deposit must be met by the payment date to hold the established short position.

MARGIN REQUIREMENTS WHEN WRITING A CALL

When an investor writes a call, the investor's margin requirement will depend greatly on whether the short call is covered. For margin purposes, a call is considered covered if the investor is long:

- The underlying stock.
- Securities convertible into the underlying stock.
- A call option with a lower exercise price and equal or longer expiration.

- A warrant with an exercise price lower than the option's exercise price.
- An escrow receipt from a bank or trust company showing the stock is on deposit and will be delivered in the case of an assignment.

If the short call is covered by any of the above positions, the option is considered covered, and no additional margin deposits will be required. If the investor is long a warrant with an exercise price that exceeds the exercise price of the call, the investor will be required to deposit the difference in the exercise price in cash to hold the position. If an investor establishes a covered call position with the underlying stock on the same day, the amount of the required deposit is reduced by the option's premium.

| **EXAMPLE** | An investor establishes the following position in a cash account: |

Buy 100 TRY at 49.

Sell 1 TRY Nov 50 call at 3.

The required cash deposit to hold 100 shares of TRY is reduced by the option's premium of $300, from $4,900 to $4,600. Alternatively, if the same position was established in a margin account, the Regulation T required deposit would also be reduced by the option's premium of $300. The Regulation T required deposit to hold the position would be reduced from $2,450 to $2,150.

If an investor writes uncovered options, the transaction must be executed in a margin account. The required margin deposit will be subject to the premium received plus a percentage of underlying stock price.

MARGIN REQUIREMENTS WHEN WRITING A PUT

The margin requirement for a short put position will depend on whether the short position is covered. A short put is considered covered if the investor has:

- Cash on deposit in an amount equal to the aggregate exercise price.
- A letter from a bank stating that an amount equal to the aggregate exercise price is on deposit.
- Established a short position in the underlying security.
- A long put with a higher exercise price and equal or longer expiration.

Because all short positions must be executed in a margin account, a short put position covered by short stock must also be established in a margin account. Short puts covered by a cash deposit or an escrow receipt may be sold in a cash account. If the short put position is uncovered, the margin requirement will be subject to the premium plus a percentage of the underlying stock price. If an investor who is short uncovered puts in a margin account is assigned, the investor may meet the margin requirement by making the required Regulation T deposit of 50% or by depositing securities with a loan value equal to 50% of the securities' market value.

MARGIN REQUIREMENTS WHEN ESTABLISHING A SPREAD

The margin requirement for an investor who establishes a spread will depend on the type of spread established. Regardless of the type of spread, all spread positions must be established in a margin account. Investors who establish debit spreads will in most cases only be required to deposit the net debit so long as the expiration of the short option does not exceed the expiration of the long option.

EXAMPLE   An investor establishes the following position:

Long 1 REW June 50 call at 5.

Short 1 REW June 60 call at 1.

The position was established for a net debit of $400. Because the investor is long the call with the lower strike price and the expiration of the short option does not exceed the expiration of the long option, the investor will only be required to deposit the net debit of $400.

If an investor establishes a credit spread or a spread where the expiration of the short option exceeds the expiration of the long option, the investor will be subject to the more stringent margin requirements of the NYSE/FINRA. A debit put spread could also be established as follows:

Long 1 REW June 80 put at 6.

Short 1 REW June 70 put at 1.

Because the investor is long the put with the higher strike price and the expiration of the short put does not exceed the expiration of the long put, the required deposit to hold this position will be limited to the net debit of $500.

Pretest

OPTION TAXATION AND MARGIN REQUIREMENTS

1. As it relates to option taxation, which of the following is true?

   a. Gains and losses on all options are short-term.

   b. Buyers of options will always have a short-term gain on the sale of an option sold at a profit.

   c. Writers of options will always have a short-term capital gain if the option expires worthless.

   d. All tax consequences for options will be factored independently from the underlying stock position.

2. An investor has held 1,000 shares of UYT for eight months. The investor paid $56.78 for the shares. The stock has increased in value to $59.76. The investor buys 10 UYT May 55 puts at $2.05. Which of the following are true?

   I. Any gain on the sale of the shares will be short-term.

   II. The investor has lowered his breakeven point on the stock.

   III. The investor has not affected his holding period for the stock.

   IV. If the puts are exercised by the investor, the sale price for tax purposes will be $57.05.

   a. I only

   b. III only

   c. II and IV

   d. III and IV

3. An investor who exercises a put must do which of the following for tax purposes?

    a. Add the put's premium to the strike price.

    b. Subtract the put's premium from the strike price.

    c. Subtract the put's premium from the price paid for the stock.

    d. Add the put's premium to the execution costs of the transaction.

4. Your customer is long 10 ERT Oct 60 calls at 3.22. The customer exercises the calls when ERT is at 62.05. For tax purposes, the customer's cost base is:

    a. $60.00.

    b. $62.05.

    c. $63.22.

    d. $65.27.

5. Your customer is long 7 ZNM April 45 puts at 3.11. The customer exercises the puts when ZNM is at 42.65. For tax purposes, the customer's proceeds are:

    a. $42.65.

    b. $45.72.

    c. $48.11.

    d. $41.89.

6. Closing transactions for option writers are taxed as which of the following?

    a. Short-term capital gains or losses

    b. Long-term capital gains or losses

    c. Ordinary income or loss

    d. None of the choices listed

7. An investor purchases 1,000 shares of IOP at 45 and purchases 10 IOP 45 puts later that day at 2.15. Which of the following are true?

   I. Any gain on the sale of the shares will be short-term.

   II. The investor has lowered his breakeven on the stock.

   III. The investor has not affected his holding period for the stock.

   IV. If the puts are exercised by the investor, the sale price for tax purposes will be $42.85.

   a. I and II

   b. III and IV

   c. II and III

   d. I and IV

8. Which of the following are true about an investor who sells a put to open?

   I. An investor may sell a put in a cash account if he has the aggregate exercise price in cash in the account.

   II. An investor who is assigned an exercise notice will have reduced his purchase price for the stock for tax purposes.

   III. If the put was sold in a margin account the investor must have cash equal to the Regulation T requirement for the stock.

   IV. Marginable securities may not be used to hold an assigned position in a margin account.

   a. I and II

   b. III and IV

   c. I, II, and III

   d. I, II, III, and IV

9. Which of the following are true for investors who engage in spread transactions?

    I. An investor who is long the spread will generally not be required to make an additional deposit past the net debit.

    II. All spreads must be established in a margin account.

    III. Additional margin requirements, if any, are determined by the NYSE/FINRA.

    IV. An investor who is short the spread will generally be required to make an additional deposit past the net credit.

    a. I and II

    b. III and IV

    c. I, II, and III

    d. I, II, III, and IV

10. Which of the following are true of options?

    I. All option transactions settle T + 1.

    II. Regulation T requires that options be paid for on T + 3.

    III. LEAPS have a loan value of 25%.

    IV. When writing a call to open, the call is covered if the investor provides an escrow receipt for the underlying shares.

    a. I and II

    b. III and IV

    c. I, II, and III

    d. I, II, III, and IV

Option Compliance and Account Supervision

INTRODUCTION

A member firm's public customer option business must be supervised by the firm in accordance with the supervision of its overall public customer business. Registered option and security futures principals (ROSFPs) designated by the firm's written supervisory procedures may supervise the member firm's option business. The ROSFP is not required to complete the security futures firm element continuing education requirement, and being designated as a ROSFP does not permit the ROSFP to supervise the member's security futures business without satisfying the security futures firm element continuing education program.

DUTIES OF THE ROSFP

The ROSFP's duties mainly focus on the supervision of the member firm's option business. The ROSFP must supervise all of the member firm's option transactions with customers. In addition, the ROSFP is responsible for:

- Developing the firm's written supervisory procedures relating to the option business.
- Developing the firm's training program for the option business.
- Reviewing discretionary account acceptance by the branch managers and other ROSFPs.

- Working with and assisting branch managers in supervising customer accounts.

The ROSFP must also design and administer supervision programs to review selected option accounts to ensure proper supervision. ROSFPs may delegate most review and supervision duties to employees (usually ROSFPs) under their direct control, but they remain responsible for all of the areas of supervision.

The ROSFP is also responsible for ensuring that the member firm's option business complies with all laws and industry regulations. The ROSFP must:

- Establish the firm's recordkeeping procedures relating to options.
- Review selected option accounts frequently.
- Establish guidelines and requirements for the firm's option advertising.
- Approve all retail communication relating to options prior to first use.
- Supervise account approval procedures.
- Supervise the creation of account approval forms.
- Develop the firm's option training program.
- Review option discretionary accounts more frequently.
- Supervise the firm's procedures for allocating assignment notices.
- Audit the firm's option compliance program.

OPTION ACCOUNT COMPLIANCE

A member firm's option business requires strict supervision from the ROFSP as well as from the firm's branch office mangers. All customer option accounts must be approved in writing by a ROSFP. Not all customers will be approved to trade options, and not all customers who are approved to trade options will be approved for more advanced or more risky option strategies. In order to determine if a customer should be approved to open an option account, the registered representative must collect as much financial information from the customer as possible. The registered representative must collect the following information from the customer:

- Full name and address
- Home and work phone numbers
- Social Security or tax ID number

- Employer, occupation, and employer's address
- Net worth and liquid net worth
- Investment objectives
- Investment experience
- Estimated annual income
- Whether the customer is employed by a bank or broker dealer
- Marital status

Based on the information collected by the agent, the ROSFP must determine if option trading is suitable for the customer. Most customers will be approved to write covered calls against long stock positions. Writing covered calls is considered to be a conservative strategy. Customers must be able to demonstrate additional levels of sophistication and financial liquidity to be approved for:

- Buying puts and calls.
- Spreads and straddles.
- Writing uncovered options.

Only customers who demonstrate the highest levels of sophistication and liquidity will be approved to write uncovered options. If a firm does allow customers to establish uncovered option positions, the firm must have specific written supervisory procedures detailing suitability requirements and minimum net equity requirements for customers. Additionally, the firm must send customers who are approved to establish uncovered option positions a special risk disclosure document relating to uncovered options prior to or at the time the first uncovered option position is established. This risk document details the fact that many uncovered option positions will have the potential for an unlimited loss. Each customer approved to trade uncovered options must have their account assigned to an options principal for review. If the branch office manager is not a ROSFP, the branch office manager may initially approve the account to trade options so long as a ROSFP also approves the account promptly. Each customer who opens an option account must be given the OCC's risk disclosure document detailing the risks and characteristics of standardized options at or prior to the time the account is approved for option trading. Should the OCC update the options disclosure document, the updated risk disclosure document must be sent to all investors who transact business in the type of options subject to the update.

Certain customers will have to provide additional information to document that option trading is allowed. Trusts, corporations, and pension plans will be required to provide additional documents to demonstrate that option trading and, if applicable, margin accounts are permitted.

Discretionary accounts will require the customer to sign a limited power of attorney. The limited power of attorney will stay in effect until the customer revokes it or dies. All discretionary option accounts must be approved in writing by two ROSFPs. The approval of the initial ROSFP must be reviewed and approved by a second ROFSP, and the account should be reviewed more frequently to ensure against churning. If the agent is going to employ a systematic option program for the discretionary account, the account holder must get a detailed description in writing of the program to be used.

Regardless of the type of account, each option order must be approved on the day that the order is entered. Option orders are not required to be approved prior to being entered by an agent but must be approved promptly by a ROSFP on the day the order is entered. Firms that use electronic or computerized surveillance may review option orders in accordance with their written supervisory procedures.

OUTSIDE ACCOUNTS FOR EMPLOYEES

FINRA Rule 3210 regarding outside accounts became effective on April 3, 2017. This rule requires that an employee of a broker dealer, exchange or the OCC who wishes to open an account at another broker dealer must obtain the employer's written permission prior to opening the account. The employee must present written notification to the broker dealer opening the account that he/she is employed by an NYSE, FINRA member firm at the time the account is opened. This rule is in effect for the employee or any of the employee's immediate family members. This rule will also require the employee to obtain the employer's written permission for accounts that were opened within 30 days of the start of employment. Excluded from this rule are accounts opened by the employee where no transactions may take place in individual securities such as accounts opened to purchase open end mutual funds, variable annuities and UITs.

OPTION AGREEMENTS

All new option accounts must be approved by the ROSFP prior to the first option trade. An option investor must sign and return the option agreement within 15 days of the account's approval to trade options. If the investor fails to return the option agreement within 15 days, no new option positions may be opened, and the investor will be limited to closing transactions only until the option agreement is signed and returned. By signing the option agreement, customers:

- Agree to notify the firm of any significant changes to their finances.
- Agree to abide by all OCC and exchange rules.
- Acknowledge that they have received and read the OCC risk disclosure document.
- Understand that any long options in the money by 1 cent or more at expiration will result in automatic exercise for the customer.
- Agree that they understand the payment, exercise, and assignment terms.

OPTION ACCOUNT SUPERVISION

Customer option accounts require strict supervision to ensure compliance with all relevant rules and to ensure that customers only trade options within their approval limits. As customers and agents manage positions, it is quite possible for a customer's account to end up with an option position that is not within the customer's approval limit.

ROSFPs must review customer accounts frequently to ensure that customers stay within their approved guidelines. It would be quite possible for a customer whose account is approved for covered calls only to end up with a naked option position if he or she sold the underlying stock without covering the short options. If a customer's account contains a position that is outside of the approval limit, written procedures must be in place detailing how to appeal to the ROSFP for an exception or the options must be covered promptly. ROSFPs must pay close attention to the relationship between customer approval limits and customer positions. When reviewing customer accounts, a ROSFP should also pay close attention to:

- Any churning or excessive commissions earned from the account.
- The amount of option positions relative to the size of the account.
- Frequent Reg. T extensions.
- Profits and losses for option trades.
- Suitability.
- Any unauthorized transactions.
- Any positions established that cannot result in a profit or that are not economical.

- Any suspicious activity (i.e., trading on inside information and front running).
- Ensure that the customer does not exceed the position limits.
- Any manipulative activity, such as capping or pegging.

It is quite possible for an investor or trader to use options to profit unduly from the knowledge of a large order and to front run the block by entering an order to buy or sell options on the stock. Similarly, a trader or investor could use options to trade on inside information and to profit unduly from non-public material information. To guard against these situations, ROSFPs will look at the account's option-trading history and the time the option order is executed relative to the block transaction or relative to the release of material information. Orders executed just prior to a block transaction or just prior to the release of material information are more suspicious than orders executed much earlier. Additionally, transactions that are outside the account's normal trading practices would raise a red flag as well. For example, if an account's normal option trade is 10 contracts and the order being examined is for 100 contracts, then that would be a cause for concern.

An option trader who has a large option position may be tempted to try to manipulate the price of the underlying stock through capping or pegging. An investor who is long a large number of put contracts may be tempted to enter orders at the end of the day to sell the underlying security to keep the stock price down. This action would be an example of capping. If the same trader was short a large number of put contracts, the trader may be tempted to enter orders at the end of the day to buy the underlying security to keep the stock price up. This would be an example of pegging. Both capping and pegging activities should be guarded against by the ROSFP and are more likely to occur in the firm's proprietary trading account or in the account of an institutional customer.

LARGE OPTION POSITION REPORTING REQUIREMENTS

Member firms are required to report certain large option positions to the OCC that are established for any account or for any group of accounts acting in concert. Firms must file a large option position report (LOPR) once the position established exceeds the filing threshold on the same side of the market. For most securities, the current filing threshold is 200 contracts on the same side of the market. Firms are required to file the initial LOPR data, as well as any changes in reportable positions, to the OCC via the LOPR submission message. Once the data is collected by the OCC, the OCC will, in turn, provide the data to the SROs. Firms are required to send their LOPR batch file to the OCC no later than 8:00 p.m. CST on or before T + 1. The date that the firm establishes, modifies, or closes an LOPR is known as the effective date. Firms are only required to send an LOPR submission to update a report when:

- There is an increase in a reported position.
- There is a decrease in a reported position.
- A reported position is closed.

If a firm reports a large option position for an account, it is required to report any changes to that position as long as the position remains above the threshold limit. If the previously reported position falls below the contract threshold, the firm only needs to file the reduction in the number of contracts in a single report. No subsequent reports are required for the position as long as the position remains below the threshold limit.

 TAKENOTE!

The test may refer to the effective date of an LOPR submission as the trade date.

CUSTOMER CONFIRMATIONS AND ACCOUNT STATEMENTS

All customers must be provided with a trade confirmation when an option order is executed. All confirmations must be sent to the customer no later than the option's settlement date, or T + 1. Option trade confirmations must disclose:

- The type of option.
- The type of transaction (i.e., buy or sell).
- The underlying security.
- The number of contracts.
- The exercise price.

- The expiration date.
- If the transaction was to open or close.
- The trade date.
- The settlement date.
- The premium and amount due or owed.
- The commission charged.
- If the firm acted as a principal or as an agent in the transaction.

A customer must receive a statement every month in which there is activity in the account. All customers must receive account statements at least quarterly when there has been no activity in the account. Examples of activity include:

- Purchases and sales.
- Dividend and interest received.
- Interest charged.
- Addition or withdrawal of cash or securities.

Customer account statements must show:

- All positions in the account.
- All activity since the last statement.
- All credit and debit balances.

Brokerage firms are required to disclose their financial condition to their clients by sending them a balance sheet every six months or upon the request of a customer with cash or securities on deposit. Customer account statements must be maintained for six years, and account statements must contain a notice requesting that the customer notify the firm of any material changes in the customer's investment objectives or financial status.

CUSTOMER COMPLAINTS

All written complaints received from a customer or from an individual acting on behalf of the customer must be reported promptly to the principal of the firm. The firm is required to:

- Maintain a copy of the complaint for 4 years in a central file.
- Maintain a record of the date the complaint was received.

- Maintain a record of the representative handling the account.
- Maintain a record of any corrective action taken.

The firm must maintain a separate customer complaint folder, even if it has not received any written customer complaints. If the firm's file contains complaints, the file must state what action was taken by the firm, if any, and it must disclose the location of the file containing any correspondence relating to the complaint. Branch offices must forward complaints to the central file within 30 days of receipt.

 TAKENOTE!

A principal is required to review all written customer complaints but there is no required time frame to respond or take action.

COMMUNICATIONS WITH THE PUBLIC

Member firms will seek to increase their business and exposure through the use of both retail and institutional communications. There are strict regulations in place in order to ensure all communications with the public adhere to industry guidelines. Some communications with the public are available to a general audience and include:

- Television/radio
- Publicly accessible websites
- Motion pictures
- Newspapers/magazines
- Telephone directory listings
- Signs/billboards
- Computer/Internet postings
- Video displays
- Other public media
- Recorded telemarketing messages

Other types of communications are offered to a targeted audience. These communications include:

- Market reports
- Password-protected websites
- Telemarketing scripts
- Form letters or e-mails (sent to more than 25 people)
- Circulars
- Research reports
- Printed materials for seminars
- Option worksheets
- Performance reports
- Prepared scripts for television or radio
- Reprints of ads

FINRA RULE 2210 COMMUNICATIONS WITH THE PUBLIC

FINRA Rule 2210 replaces the advertising and sales literature rules previously used to regulate member communications with the public. FINRA Rule 2210 streamlines member communication rules and reduces the number of communication categories from six to three. The three categories of member communication are retail, institutional, and correspondence.

RETAIL COMMUNICATION

Retail communication is defined as any written communication distributed or made available to 25 or more retail investors in a 30-day period. The communication may be distributed in hard copy or in electronic formats. The definition of a retail investor is any investor who does not meet the definition of an institutional investor. Retail communications now contain all components of advertising and sales literature. All retail communications must be approved by a registered principal prior to first use. The publication of a post in a chat room or other online forum will not require the prior approval of a principal so long as such post does not promote the business of the member firm and does not provide investment advice. Additionally, generic advertising will also be exempt from the prior approval requirements. All retail communication must be maintained by the member for three years. If the member firm is a new member firm that has been in existence for less than 12 months based on the firm's approval date in the central registration depository (CRD), the member must file all retail communications with FINRA 10 days prior to its first use unless the communication has been previously filed and contains no material changes or has been filed by another member, such as an investment company or ETF sponsor. Member firms who have been established for more than 12 months may file retail communications with FINRA 10 days after the communication is first used. Investment companies, ETF sponsors, and retail communications regarding variable annuities must be filed 10 days prior to first use if the communication contains non standardized performance rankings. Should FINRA determine that a member firm is making false or misleading statements in its retail communications with the public, FINRA may require the member to file with the association all of its retail communication with the public 10 days prior to its first use.

INSTITUTIONAL COMMUNICATIONS

Institutional communication is defined as any written communication distributed or made available exclusively to institutional investors. The communication may be distributed in hard copy or in electronic formats. Institutional communications do not have to be approved by a principal prior to first use so long as the member has established policies and procedures regarding the use of institutional communications and has trained its employees on the proper use of institutional communication. Institutional communication is also exempt from FINRA's filing requirement, but like retail communications, it must be maintained by a member for 3 years. If the member believes that the institutional communication or any part thereof may be seen by even a single retail investor, the communication must be handled as all other retail communication and is subject to the same approval and filing requirements as if it was retail communication. An institutional investor is a person or firm that trades securities for his or her own account or for the account of others. Institutional investors are generally limited to large financial companies. Because of their size and sophistication, fewer protective laws cover institutional investors. It is important to note that there is no minimum size for an institutional account. Institutional investors include:

- Broker dealers
- Investment advisers
- Investment companies
- Insurance companies

- Banks
- Trusts
- Savings and loans
- Government agencies
- Employment benefit plans with more than 100 participants
- Any non-natural person with more than $50,000,000 in assets

CORRESPONDENCE COMMUNICATIONS

Correspondence consists of electronic and written communications between the member and up to 25 retail investors in a 30-calendar-day period. With the increase in acceptance of e-mail as business communication, it would be impractical for a member to review all correspondence between the member and a customer. The member instead may set up procedures to review a sample of all correspondence, both electronic and hard copy. If the member reviews only a sample of the correspondence, the member must train its associated people on the firm's procedures relating to correspondence and must document the training and ensure the procedures are followed. Even though the member is not required to review all correspondence, the member must still retain all correspondence. The member should, where practical, review all incoming hard copy correspondence. Letters received by the firm could contain cash, checks, securities, or complaints.

All retail communications relating to options must be approved by the firm's designated ROSFP before it is first used. Educational material relating to options must inform the reader how to obtain information about the risks of option investing. All communication with the public relating to options that mentions the potential profitability of option investing must clearly balance those statements by discussing the potential risks associated with option investing. If the communication cites past recommendations, all recommendations in that option type (calls, puts) for the past 12 months must be cited. The general market conditions must also be disclosed, and any mention or calculation of annualized returns must be based on at least 60 days. Supporting documentation for past performance must be made available upon request. All retail communications relating to options and educational material must be submitted to the exchange 10 days prior to its first use and should contain information about how to obtain the OCC's risk disclosure document. All communications relating to options must be maintained by the firm for 3 years total and in a readily accessible location for 2 years.

Pretest

OPTION COMPLIANCE AND ACCOUNT SUPERVISION

1. An investor opening an option account would least likely be approved to do which of the following?
   a. Naked calls
   b. Naked puts
   c. Long straddles
   d. Short straddles

2. Your existing customer has just been approved by your firm's ROSFP to trade options. How long does the customer have to return the signed option agreement?
   a. 5 days
   b. 45 days
   c. 15 days
   d. 30 days

3. A branch office that receives a written complaint has how long to forward the complaint to the firm's central complaint file?
   a. 5 days
   b. 10 days
   c. 15 days
   d. 30 days

4. Which of the following are required for an employee wishing to open an option account with another member firm?

   I. Employer's written permission
   II. Duplicate confirmations sent to employer
   III. Duplicate statements sent to employer
   IV. Signed option agreement

   a. I and II
   b. III and IV
   c. I, II, and IV
   d. I, II, III, and IV

5. Which of the following are duties of the ROSFP?

   I. Developing the written supervisory procedures for options
   II. Reviewing selected discretionary option accounts accepted by branch managers
   III. Supervising the firm's option assignments
   IV. Establishing option recordkeeping procedures

   a. I only
   b. III only
   c. I, II, and III
   d. I, II, III, and IV

6. Which of the following acknowledgments are contained in the option agreement?

   I. The customer agrees to abide by all OCC and exchange rules.
   II. The customer understands the terms under which an automatic exercise will occur.
   III. The customer agrees to notify the firm of any material financial change.
   IV. The customer acknowledges the receipt of the risk disclosure document.

   a. I and IV
   b. II and III
   c. I, II, and III
   d. I, II, III, and IV

7. Which of the following investors would be most likely to engage in capping?

   I. An investor with long calls

   II. An investor with long puts

   III. An investor with short calls

   IV. An investor with short puts

   a. I only

   b. II only

   c. II and III

   d. I and IV

Answer Keys

CHAPTER 1: OPTION BASICS

1. (B) Your maximum gain when you sell an option with no other positions in the account is always the premium received.

2. (B) The investor's breakeven point was 56.50, which was found by subtracting the premium from the put's strike price. The stock closed at 56.05, so the investor lost 45 cents per share, or $90 for the position.

3. (D) I is incorrect in that an option is a contract between two parties, which determines the time and price at which a security may be bought or sold.

4. (C) Call sellers and put buyers are both bearish. They want the value of the stock to fall.

5. (B) The OCC (Options Clearing Corporation) issues all standardized options.

6. (D) The investor made $3,900. The options are worth $7,000 at expiration. The investor paid $3,100. Therefore, the profit is $3,900.

7. (A) The options are at the money and have no intrinsic value.

8. (B) Only the XYZ March 55 put is in the money with XYZ at 52.50.

9. (A) A call option is in the money when the stock price is higher than the strike price. The time value of an option is the amount by which the option's premium exceeds the intrinsic value. The option is in the money by $1.10, and the time value of the option is $3.25.

10. (B) The investor closes out the position at its intrinsic value of $4 with a closing purchase. The investor sold the puts at $5.30. Therefore, the investor made $1.30 per share, or $1,300 for the entire position.

CHAPTER 2: OPTION STRATEGIES

1. (B) A debit call spread and a credit put spread are both bullish. Straddles are neither bullish nor bearish.
2. (B) To gain some protection and take in premium income for a 10,000-share position, you would sell 100 XYZ Oct 45 calls.
3. (A) With a long straddle, the maximum gain is unlimited because the investor owns the calls.
4. (B) This is a credit spread; the investor wants the options to expire and the spread in the premiums to narrow.
5. (D) On a credit spread, the maximum gain is always the credit received.
6. (D) An investor selling stock short will gain the maximum protection by buying calls.
7. (A) A diagonal spread consists of a long and short option of the same type with different strike prices and expiration months.
8. (C) An investor who is long stock with a protective put and an investor who is long a straddle have a maximum gain that is unlimited.
9. (A) An investor who is long a spread will realize a loss if the options expire or the spread narrows.
10. (C) An investor who sells a straddle against a long stock position will have all of the choices listed except less risk than an investor who sells covered calls.

CHAPTER 3: INDEX, INTEREST RATE, AND CURRENCY OPTIONS

1. (C) The option is for $100,000 par value. The investor will receive accrued interest plus the exercise price of $103,000 upon delivery of the bond.
2. (A) If you think that bond prices are going down, you would want to buy rate-based calls and/or price-based puts.
3. (C) U.S. importers will always buy calls on the foreign currency to hedge themselves. The dollar-based answer is always wrong. There are no options trading on the U.S. dollar in the United States.
4. (B) Capped index options trade like spreads and are automatically exercised if they go 30 points in the money.
5. (B) It is not possible to write a rate-based covered call. Rate-based options are based on T-bills that have not been issued yet.

6. (B) The investor would pay $1,250. The quote of 1.08 = 1 8/32% or 1.25% of $100,000 = $1,250.

7. (D) All of the choices are false except that the U.S. dollar is the base currency for all foreign currency options.

8. (D) The Japanese yen is quoted in hundredths of a cent and the decimal point for the quote must be moved four places to the left.

9. (C) Currency options expire on the third Friday.

10. (C) Of the choices listed, only the price-based call settles in the delivery of the underlying asset. All of the other options settle in cash.

CHAPTER 4: THE OPTIONS MARKETPLACE

1. (A) The OCC is wholly owned by the exchanges.

2. (C) Order book officials are employees of the exchange and may not trade for their own accounts.

3. (D) Equity options that are exercised will result in the delivery of the underlying stock in 3 business days.

4. (B) A put writer who has been assigned the stock on the Friday before the ex dividend date would be entitled to receive the dividend because he would be an owner of record on the record date. The stock that was put to him would settle regular way in 3 business days.

5. (D) All exercise notices must be sent by 4:30 p.m. CST on the Friday prior to expiration.

6. (B) If a stock splits 2:1, the investor will now own two contracts with a lower exercise price both covering 100 shares.

7. (B) Assignments from the OCC will be done on a random basis only.

8. (A) The OCC will assign an exercise notice to a broker dealer who has a customer who is short the option. The broker dealer then must assign the exercise notice to a customer who is short the option on a random basis. The OCC is not a self-regulatory organization.

9. (C) Options expire at 10:59 p.m. CST on the third Friday. Equity options cease trading at 4:00 p.m. EST on the day of expiration.

10. (A) The OCC is not involved in option trading rotations, and the puts with the highest strike price are the first puts quoted in the trading rotation.

CHAPTER 5: OPTION TAXATION AND MARGIN REQUIREMENTS

1. (C) Writers of options will always have a short-term capital gain if the option expires worthless, regardless of whether the option involved is a traditional option or LEAPS. Buyers of LEAPS can have a long-term capital gain

2. (A) The investor has purchased puts to protect a stock position held less than 12 months. Therefore, any gain or loss will be short-term. All of the other choices are false.

3. (B) The investor must subtract the put's premium from the put's strike price.

4. (C) To determine the customer's cost base you must add the option's premium to the exercise price. In this case, 60 + 3.22 = $63.22.

5. (D) With a put option, you must subtract the option's premium from the strike price. In this case, 45 − 3.11 = $41.89.

6. (A) Closing transactions for option writers are treated as short-term capital gains or losses.

7. (B) The investor has not affected his holding period on the stock because the puts were purchased on the same day. The order ticket for the puts would need to indicate that the puts were protective or married puts. The sales price for the stock would be $42.85 if the puts are exercised by the investor.

8. (C) All of the choices listed are true regarding an investor who sells puts to open except option IV. An investor can use marginable securities with a loan value equal to the Reg. T requirement to hold the position so long as the puts were sold in a margin account.

9. (D) All of the choices are true for investors who engage in spread transactions.

10. (D) All of the choices listed are true regarding option transactions.

CHAPTER 6: OPTION COMPLIANCE AND ACCOUNT SUPERVISION

1. (A) An investor would be least likely to be approved to sell naked calls.

2. (C) A customer must return the signed option agreement within 15 days of the account's approval to trade options.

3. (D) A branch office must forward all written customer complaints to the central complaint file within 30 days.

4. (D) All of the answers listed are required for an employee of another member that opens an option account with another firm.

5. (D) The ROSFP must develop the firm's written supervisory material, review discretionary account approval by branch managers, supervise assignments, and establish recordkeeping procedures.

6. (D) All of the choices listed are acknowledged and agreed to by customers when they sign the option agreement.

7. (C) Investors who are short calls and long puts would be most likely to engage in capping. Capping is trying to keep a stock price down.

Glossary of Exam Terms

A

AAA/Aaa	The highest investment-grade rating for bond issuers awarded by Standard & Poor's and Moody's ratings agencies.
acceptance waiver and consent (AWAC)	A process used when a respondent does not contest an allegation made by FINRA. The respondent accepts the findings without admitting any wrongdoing and agrees to accept any penalty for the violation.
account executive (AE)	An individual who is duly licensed to represent a broker dealer in securities transactions or investment banking business. Also known as a registered representative.
accredited investor	Any individual or institution that meets one or more of the following: (1) a net worth exceeding $1 million, excluding the primary residence, or (2) is single and has an annual income of $200,000 or more or $300,000 jointly with a spouse.
accretion	An accounting method used to step up an investor's cost base for a bond purchased at a discount.
accrued interest	The portion of a debt securities future interest payment that has been earned by the seller of the security. The purchaser must pay this amount of accrued interest to the seller at the time of the transaction's settlement. Interest accrues from the date of the last interest payment date up to, but not including, the transaction's settlement date.
accumulation stage	The period during which an annuitant is making contributions to an annuity contract.
accumulation unit	A measure used to determine the annuitant's proportional ownership interest in the insurance company's separate account during the accumulation

stage. During the accumulation stage, the number of accumulation units owned by the annuitant changes and their value varies.

acid-test ratio	A measure of corporate liquidity found by subtracting inventory from current assets and dividing the result by the current liabilities.
ACT	*See* Automated Comparison Transaction (ACT) service.
ad valorem tax	A tax based on the value of the subject property.
adjusted basis	The value assigned to an asset after all deductions or additions for improvements have been taken into consideration.
adjusted gross income (AGI)	An accounting measure employed by the IRS to help determine tax liability. AGI = earned income + investment income (portfolio income) + capital gains + net passive income.
administrator	(1) An individual authorized to oversee the liquidation of an intestate decedent's estate. (2) An individual or agency that administers securities' laws within a state.
ADR/ADS	*See* American depositary receipt (ADR).
advance/decline line	Measures the health of the overall market by calculating advancing issues and subtracting the number of declining issues.
advance refunding	The early refinancing of municipal securities. A new issue of bonds is sold to retire the old issue at its first available call date or maturity.
advertisement	Any material that is distributed by a broker dealer or issuer for the purpose of increasing business or public awareness for the firm or issuer. The broker dealer or issuer must distribute advertisements to an audience that is not controlled. Advertisements are distributed through any of the following: newspapers/magazines, radio, TV, billboards, telephone.
affiliate	An individual who owns 10% or more of the company's voting stock. In the case of a direct participation program (DPP), this is anyone who controls the partnership or is controlled by the partnership.
agency issue	A debt security issued by any authorized entity of the U.S. government. The debt security is an obligation of the issuing entity, not an obligation of the U.S. government (with the exception of Ginnie Mae and the Federal Import Export Bank issues).
agency transaction	A transaction made by a firm for the benefit of a customer. The firm merely executes a customer's order and charges a fee for the service, which is known as a commission.
agent	A firm or an individual who executes securities transactions for customers and charges a service fee known as a commission. Also known as a broker.

aggregate indebtedness	The total amount of the firm's customer-related debts.
allied member	An owner-director or 5% owner of an NYSE member firm. Allied members may not trade on the floor.
all-or-none (AON) order	A non-time-sensitive order that stipulates that the customer wants to buy or sell all of the securities in the order.
all-or-none underwriting	A type of underwriting that states that the issuer wants to sell all of the securities being offered or none of the securities being offered. The proceeds from the issue will be held in escrow until all securities are sold.
alpha	A measure of the projected change in the security's price as a result of fundamental factors relating only to that company.
alternative minimum tax (AMT)	A method used to calculate the tax liability for some high-income earners that adds back the deductions taken for certain tax preference items.
AMBAC Indemnity Corporation	Insures the interest and principal payments for municipal bonds.
American depositary receipt (ADR)/ American depositary security (ADS)	A receipt representing the beneficial ownership of foreign securities being held in trust overseas by a foreign branch of a U.S. bank. ADRs/ADSs facilitate the trading and ownership of foreign securities and trade in the United States on an exchange or in the over-the-counter markets.
American Stock Exchange (AMEX)	An exchange located in New York using the dual-auction method and specialist system to facilitate trading in stocks, options, exchange-traded funds, and portfolios. AMEX was acquired by the NYSE Euronext and is now part of NYSE Alternext.
amortization	An accounting method that reduces the value of an asset over its projected useful life. Also the way that loan principal is systematically paid off over the life of a loan.
annual compliance review	All firms must hold at least one compliance meeting per year with all of its agents.
annuitant	An individual who receives scheduled payments from an annuity contract.
annuitize	A process by which an individual converts from the accumulation stage to the payout stage of an annuity contract. This is accomplished by exchanging accumulation units for annuity units. Once a payout option is selected, it cannot be changed.
annuity	A contract between an individual and an insurance company that is designed to provide the annuitant with lifetime income in exchange for either a lump sum or periodic deposits into the contract.

annuity unit	An accounting measure used to determine an individual's proportionate ownership of the separate account during the payout stage of the contract. The number of annuity units owned by an individual remains constant, and their value, which may vary, is used to determine the amount of the individual's annuity payment.
appreciation	An asset's increase in value over time.
arbitrage	An investment strategy used to profit from market inefficiencies.
arbitration	A forum provided by both the NYSE and FINRA to resolve disputes between two parties. Only a public customer may not be forced to settle a dispute through arbitration. The public customer must agree to arbitration in writing. All industry participants must settle disputes through arbitration.
ask	*See* offer.
assessed value	A base value assigned to property for the purpose of determining tax liability.
assessment	An additional amount of taxes due as a result of a municipal project that the homeowner benefits from. Also an additional call for capital by a direct participation program.
asset	Anything of value owned by an individual or a corporation.
asset allocation fund	A mutual fund that spreads its investments among different asset classes (i.e., stocks, bonds, and other investments) based on a predetermined formula.
assignee	A person to whom the ownership of an asset is being transferred.
assignment	(1) The transfer of ownership or rights through a signature. (2) The notification given to investors who are short an option that the option holder has exercised its right and they must now meet their obligations as detailed in the option contract.
associated person	Any individual under the control of a broker dealer, issuer, or bank, including employees, officers, and directors, as well as those individuals who control or have common control of a broker dealer, issuer, or bank.
assumed interest rate (AIR)	(1) A benchmark used to determine the minimum rate of return that must be realized by a variable annuity's separate account during the payout phase in order to keep the annuitant's payments consistent. (2) In the case of a variable life insurance policy, the minimum rate of return that must be achieved in order to maintain the policy's variable death benefit.
at-the-close order	An order that stipulates that the security is to be bought or sold only at the close of the market, or as close to the close as is reasonable, or not at all.
at the money	A term used to describe an option when the underlying security price is equal to the exercise price of the option.

at-the-opening order	An order that stipulates that the security is to be bought or sold only at the opening of the market, or as close to the opening as is reasonable, or not at all.
auction market	The method of trading employed by stock exchanges that allows buyers and sellers to compete with one another in a centralized location.
authorized stock	The maximum number of shares that a corporation can sell in an effort to raise capital. The number of authorized shares may only be changed by a vote of the shareholders.
Automated Comparison Transaction (ACT) service	ACT is the service that clears and locks Nasdaq trades.
average cost	A method used to determine the cost of an investment for an investor who has made multiple purchases of the same security at different times and prices. An investor's average cost may be used to determine a cost base for tax purposes or to evaluate the profitability of an investment program, such as dollar-cost averaging. Average cost is determined by dividing the total dollars invested by the number of shares purchased.
average price	A method used to determine the average price paid by an investor for a security that has been purchased at different times and prices, such as through dollar-cost averaging. An investor's average price is determined by dividing the total of the purchase prices by the number of purchases.

B

BBB/Baa	The lowest ratings assigned by Standard & Poor's and Moody's for debt in the investment-grade category.
back-end load	A mutual fund sales charge that is assessed upon the redemption of the shares. The amount of the sales charge to be assessed upon redemption decreases the longer the shares are held. Also known as a contingent deferred sales charge.
backing away	The failure of an over-the-counter market maker to honor firm quotes. It is a violation of FINRA rules.
balanced fund	A mutual fund whose investment policy requires that the portfolio's holdings are diversified among asset classes and invested in common and preferred stock, bonds, and other debt instruments. The exact asset distribution among the asset classes will be predetermined by a set formula that is designed to balance out the investment return of the fund.
balance of payments	The net balance of all international transactions for a country in a given time.

balance of trade	The net flow of goods into or out of a country for a given period. Net exports result in a surplus or credit; net exports result in a deficit or net debit.
balance sheet	A corporate report that shows a company's financial condition at the time the balance sheet was created.
balance sheet equation	Assets = liabilities + shareholders equity.
balloon maturity	A bond maturity schedule that requires the largest portion of the principal to be repaid on the last maturity date.
bankers' acceptance (BA)	A letter of credit that facilitates foreign trade. BAs are traded in the money market and have a maximum maturity of 270 days.
basis	The cost that is assigned to an asset.
basis book	A table used to calculate bond prices for bonds quoted on a yield basis and to calculate yields for bonds quoted on a price basis.
basis point	Measures a bond's yield; 1 basis point is equal to 1/100 of 1%.
basis quote	A bond quote based on the bond's yield.
bearer bond	A bond that is issued without the owner's name being registered on the bond certificate or the books of the issuer. Whoever has possession of (bears) the certificate is deemed to be the rightful owner.
bearish	An investor's belief that prices will decline.
bear market	A market condition that is characterized by continuing falling prices and a series of lower lows in overall prices.
best efforts underwriting	A type of underwriting that does not guarantee the issuer that any of its securities will be sold.
beta	A measure of a security's or portfolio's volatility relative to the market as a whole. A security or portfolio whose beta is greater than 1 will experience a greater change in price than overall market prices. A security or portfolio with a beta of less than 1 will experience a price change that is less than the price changes realized by the market as a whole.
bid	A price that an investor or broker dealer is willing to pay for a security. It is also a price at which an investor may sell a security immediately and the price at which a market maker will buy a security.
blind pool	A type of direct participation program where less than 75% of the assets to be acquired have been identified.
block trade	A trade involving 10,000 shares or market value of over $200,000.
blotter	A daily record of broker dealer transactions.
blue chip stock	Stock of a company whose earnings and dividends are stable regardless of the economy.

Blue List	A daily publication of municipal bond offerings and secondary market interest.
blue sky	A term used to describe the state registration process for a security offering.
blue-sky laws	Term used to describe the state-based laws enacted under the Uniform Securities Act.
board broker	*See* order book official.
board of directors	A group of directors elected by the stockholders of a corporation to appoint and oversee corporate management.
Board of Governors	The governing body of FINRA. The board is made up of 27 members elected by FINRA's membership and the board itself.
bona fide quote	*See* firm quote.
bond	The legal obligation of a corporation or government to repay the principal amount of debt along with interest at a predetermined schedule.
bond anticipation note	Short-term municipal financing sold in anticipation of long-term financing.
bond buyer indexes	A group of yield-based municipal bond indexes published daily in the *Daily Bond Buyer*.
bond counsel	An attorney for the issuer of municipal securities who renders the legal opinion.
bond fund	A fund whose portfolio is made up of debt instruments issued by corporations, governments, and/or their agencies. The fund's investment objective is usually current income.
bond interest coverage ratio	A measure of the issuer's liquidity. It demonstrates how many times the issuer's earnings will cover its bond interest expense.
bond quotes	Corporate and government bond quotes are based on a percentage of par. Municipal bonds are usually quoted on a yield-to-maturity basis.
bond rating	A rating that assesses the financial soundness of issuers and their ability to make interest and principal payments in a timely manner. Standard & Poor's and Moody's are the two largest ratings agencies. Issuers must request and pay for the service to rate their bonds.
bond ratio	A measure used to determine how much of the corporation's capitalization was obtained through the issuance of bonds.
bond swap	The sale and purchase of two different bonds to allow the investor to claim a loss on the bond being sold without violating wash sale rules.
book entry	Securities that are issued in book entry form do not offer any physical certificates as evidence of ownership. The owner's name is registered on the books of the issuer, and the only evidence of ownership is the trade confirmation.

book value	A corporation's book value is the theoretical liquidation value of the company. Book value is in theory what someone would be willing to pay for the entire company.
book value per bond	A measure used to determine the amount of the corporation's tangible value for each bond issued.
book value per share	Used to determine the tangible value of each common share. It is found by subtracting intangible assets and the par value of preferred stock from the corporation's total net worth and dividing that figure by the number of common shares outstanding.
branch office	A branch office of a member firm is required to display the name of the member firm and is any office in which the member conducts securities business outside of its main office.
breadth	A measure of the broad market's health. It measures how many stocks are increasing and how many are declining.
breakdown	A technical term used to describe the price action of a security when it falls below support to a lower level and into a new trading range.
breakeven point	The point at which the value of a security or portfolio is exactly equal to the investor's cost for that security or portfolio.
breakout	A technical term used to describe the price action of a security when it increases past resistance to a higher level and into a new trading range.
breakpoint sale	The practice of selling mutual fund shares in dollar amounts that are just below the point where an investor would be entitled to a sales charge reduction. A breakpoint sale is designed for the purpose of trying to earn a larger commission. This is a violation of the Rules of Fair Practice and should never be done.
breakpoint schedule	A breakpoint schedule offers mutual fund investors reduced sales charges for larger dollar investments.
broad-based index	An index that represents a large cross-section of the market as a whole. The price movement of the index reflects the price movement of a large portion of the market, such as the S&P 500 or the Wilshire 5000.
broker	*See* agent.
broker dealer	A person or firm who buys and sells securities for its own account and for the accounts of others. When acting as a broker or agent for a customer, the broker dealer is merely executing the customer's orders and charging the customer a fee known as a commission. When acting as a dealer or principal, the broker dealer is trading for its own account and participating in the customer's transaction by taking the other side of the trade and charging the customer

a markup or markdown. A firm also is acting as a principal or dealer when it is trading for its own account and making markets in OTC securities.

broker's broker	(1) A municipal bond dealer who specializes in executing orders for other dealers who are not active in the municipal bond market. (2) A specialist on the exchange executing orders for other members or an OTC market.
bullish	An investor who believes that the price of a security or prices as a whole will rise is said to be bullish.
bull market	A market condition that is characterized by rising prices and a series of higher highs.
business cycle	The normal economic pattern that is characterized by four stages: expansion, peak, contraction, and trough. The business cycle constantly repeats itself and the economy is always in flux.
business day	The business day in the securities industry is defined as the time when the financial markets are open for trading.
buyer's option	A settlement option that allows the buyer to determine when the transaction will settle.
buy in	An order executed in the event of a customer's or firm's failure to deliver the securities it sold. The buyer repurchases the securities in the open market and charges the seller for any loss.
buying power	The amount of money available to buy securities.
buy stop order	A buy stop order is used to protect against a loss or to protect a profit on a short sale of stock.

C

call	(1) A type of option that gives the holder the right to purchase a specified amount of the underlying security at a stated price for a specified period of time. (2) The act of exercising a call option.
callable bond	A bond that may be called in or retired by the issuer prior to its maturity date.
callable preferred	A preferred share issued with a feature allowing the issuing corporation to retire it under certain conditions.
call date	A specific date after which the securities in question become callable by the issuer.
call feature	A condition attached to some bonds and preferred stocks that allows the issuer to call in or redeem the securities prior to their maturity date and according to certain conditions.

call price	The price that will be paid by the issuer to retire the callable securities in question. The call price is usually set at a price above the par value of the bond or preferred stock, which is the subject of the call.
call protection	A period of time, usually right after the securities' issuance, when the securities may not be called by the issuer. Call protection usually ranges from 5 to 10 years.
call provision	*See* call feature.
call risk	The risk borne by the owner of callable securities that may require that the investor accept a lower rate of return once the securities have been called. Callable bonds and preferred stock are more likely to be called when interest rates are low or are falling.
call spread	An option position consisting of one long and one short call on the same underlying security with different strike prices, expirations, or both.
call writer	An investor who has sold a call.
capital	Money and assets available to use in an attempt to earn more money or to accumulate more assets.
capital appreciation	An increase in an asset's value over time.
capital assets	Tangible assets, including securities, real estate, equipment, and other assets, owned for the long term.
capital gain	A profit realized on the sale of an asset at a price that exceeds its cost.
capitalization	The composition of a company's financial structure. It is the sum of paid-in capital + paid-in surplus + long-term debt + retained earnings.
capital loss	A loss realized on the sale of an asset at a price that is lower than its cost.
capital market	The securities markets that deal in equity and debt securities with more than 1 year to maturity.
capital risk	The risk that the value of an asset will decline and cause an investor to lose all or part of the invested capital.
capital stock	The sum of the par value of all of a corporation's outstanding common and preferred stock.
capital structure	*See* capitalization.
capital surplus	The amount of money received by an issuer in excess of the par value of the stock at the time of its initial sale to the public.
capped index option	An index option that trades like a spread and is automatically exercised if it goes 30 points in the money.
capping	A manipulative practice of selling stock to depress the price.

carried interest	A sharing arrangement for an oil and gas direct participation program where the general partner shares in the tangible drilling costs with the limited partners.
cash account	An account in which the investor must deposit the full purchase price of the securities by the fifth business day after the trade date. The investor is not required by industry regulations to sign anything to open a cash account.
cash assets ratio	The most liquid measure of a company's solvency. The cash asset ratio is found by dividing cash and equivalents by current liabilities.
cash dividend	The distribution of corporate profits to shareholders of record. Cash dividends must be declared by the company's board of directors.
cash equivalent	Short-term liquid securities that can quickly be converted into cash. Money market instruments and funds are the most common examples.
cash flow	A company's cash flow equals net income plus depreciation.
cashiering department	The department in a brokerage firm that is responsible for the receipt and delivery of cash and securities.
cash management bill	Short-term federal financing issued in minimum denominations of $10 million.
cash settlement	A transaction that settles for cash requires the delivery of the securities from the seller as well as the delivery of cash from the buyer on the same day of the trade. A trade done for cash settles the same day.
catastrophe call	The redemption of a bond by an issuer due to the destruction of the facility that was financed by the issue. Issuers will carry insurance to cover such events and to pay off the bondholders.
certificate of deposit (CD)	An unsecured promissory note issued as evidence of ownership of a time deposit that has been guaranteed by the issuing bank.
certificates of accrual on Treasury securities	Zero-coupon bonds issued by brokerage firms and collateralized by Treasury securities.
change	The difference between the current price and the previous day's closing price.
Chicago Board of Trade (CBOT)	A commodity exchange that provides a marketplace for agricultural and financial futures.
Chicago Board Options Exchange (CBOE)	The premier option exchange in the United States for listed options.
Chinese wall	The physical separation that is required between investment banking and trading and retail divisions of a brokerage firm. Now known as a firewall.

churning	Executing transactions that are excessive in their frequency or size in light of the resources of the account for the purpose of generating commissions. Churning is a violation of the Rules of Fair Practice.
class A share	A mutual fund share that charges a front-end load.
class B share	A mutual fund share that charges a back-end load.
class C share	A mutual fund share that charges a level load.
class D share	A mutual fund share that charges a level load and a back-end load.
classical economics	A theory stating that the economy will do the best when the government does not interfere.
clearing firm	A firm that carries its customers' cash and securities and/or provides the service to customers of other firms.
clearinghouse	An agency that guarantees and settles futures and option transactions.
close	The last price at which a security traded for the day.
closed-end indenture	A bond indenture that will not allow additional bonds to be issued with the same claim on the issuer's assets.
closed-end investment company	A management company that issues a fixed number of shares to investors in a managed portfolio and whose shares are traded in the secondary market.
closing date	The date when sales of interest in a direct participation plan will cease.
closing purchase	An order executed to close out a short option position.
Code of Arbitration Procedure	The FINRA bylaw that provides for a forum for dispute resolution relating to industry matters. All industry participants must arbitrate in public and the customer must agree to arbitration in writing.
Code of Procedure	The FINRA bylaw that sets guidelines for the investigation of trade practice complaints and alleged rule violations.
coincident indicator	An economic indicator that moves simultaneously with the movement of the underlying economy.
collateral	Assets pledged to a lender. If the borrower defaults, the lender will take possession of the collateral.
collateral trust certificate	A bond backed by the pledge of securities the issuer owns in another entity.
collateralized mortgage obligation (CMO)	A corporate debt security that is secured by an underlying pool of mortgages.
collection ratio	A measure of a municipality's ability to collect the taxes it has assessed.
collect on delivery (COD)	A method of trade settlement that requires the physical delivery of the securities to receive payment.

combination	An option position with a call and put on the same underlying security with different strike prices and expiration months on both.
combination fund	A mutual fund that tries to achieve growth and current income by combining portfolios of common stock with portfolios of high-yielding equities.
combination preferred stock	A preferred share with multiple features, such as cumulative and participating.
combination privileges	A feature offered by a mutual fund family that allows an investor to combine two simultaneous purchases of different portfolios in order to receive a reduced sales charge on the total amount invested.
combined account	A margin account that contains both long and short positions.
commercial paper	Short-term unsecured promissory notes issued by large financially stable corporations to obtain short-term financing. Commercial paper does not pay interest and is issued at a discount from its face value. All commercial paper matures in 270 days or less and matures at its face value.
commingling	A FINRA violation resulting from the mixing of customer and firm assets in the same account.
commission	A fee charged by a broker or agent for executing a securities transaction.
commission house broker	A floor broker who executes orders for the firm's account and for the accounts of the firm's customers on an exchange.
common stock	A security that represents the ownership of a corporation. Common stockholders vote to elect the board of directors and to institute major corporate policies.
common stock ratio	A measure of how much of a company's capitalization was obtained through the sale of common stock. The ratio is found by summing the par value of the common stock, excess paid in capital, and retained earnings, and then dividing that number by the total capitalization.
competitive bid underwriting	A method of underwriter selection that solicits bids from multiple underwriters. The underwriter submitting the best terms will be awarded the issue.
compliance department	The department of a broker dealer that ensures that the firm adheres to industry rules and regulations.
concession	The amount of an underwriting discount that is allocated to a syndicate member or a selling group member for selling new securities.
conduct rules	The Rules of Fair Practice.
conduit theory	The IRS classification that allows a regulated investment company to avoid paying taxes on investment income it distributes to its shareholders.

confirmation	The receipt for a securities transaction that must be sent to all customers either on or before the completion of a transaction. The confirmation must show the trade date, settlement date, and total amount due to or from the customer. A transaction is considered to be complete on settlement date.
consolidated tape	The consolidated tape A displays transactions for NYSE securities that take place on the NYSE, all regional exchanges, and the third markets. The consolidated tape B reports transactions for AMEX stocks that take place on the American Stock Exchange, all regional exchanges, and in the third market.
consolidation	A chart pattern that results from a narrowing of a security's trading range.
constant dollar plan	An investment plan designed to keep a specific amount of money invested in the market regardless of the market's condition. An investor will sell when the value of the account rises and buy when the value of the account falls.
constant ratio plan	An investment plan designed to keep the investor's portfolio invested at a constant ratio of equity and debt securities.
construction loan note	A short-term municipal note designed to provide financing for construction projects.
constructive receipt	The time when the IRS determines that the taxpayer has effectively received payment.
consumer price index (CPI)	A price-based index made up of a basket of goods and services that are used by consumers in their daily lives. An increase in the CPI indicates a rise in overall prices, while a decline in the index represents a fall in overall prices.
consumption	A term used to describe the purchase of newly produced household goods.
contemporaneous trader	A trader who enters an order on the other side of the market at the same time as a trader with inside information enters an order. Contemporaneous traders can sue traders who act on inside information to recover losses.
contingent deferred sales charge	*See* back-end load.
contraction	A period of declining economic output. Also known as a recession.
contractual plan	A mutual fund accumulation plan under which the investor agrees to contribute a fixed sum of money over time. If the investor does not complete or terminates the contract early, the investor may be subject to penalties.
control	The ability to influence the actions of an organization or individual.
control person	A director or officer of an issuer or broker dealer or a 10% stockholder of a corporation.
control stock	Stock that is acquired or owned by an officer, director, or person owning 10% or more of the outstanding stock of a company.

conversion price	The set price at which a convertible security may be exchanged for another security.
conversion privilege	The right offered to a mutual fund investor that allows the investor to move money between different portfolios offered by the same mutual fund family without paying another sales charge.
conversion ratio	The number of shares that can be received by the holder of a convertible security if it were converted into the underlying common stock.
convertible bond	A bond that may be converted or exchanged for common shares of the corporation at a predetermined price.
convertible preferred stock	A preferred stock that may be converted or exchanged for common shares of the corporation at a predetermined price.
cooling-off period	The period of time between the filing of a registration statement and its effective date. During this time, the SEC is reviewing the registration statement and no sales may take place. The cooling-off period is at least 20 days.
coordination	A method of securities registration during which a new issue is registered simultaneously at both the federal and state levels.
corporate account	An investment account for the benefit of a company that requires a corporate resolution listing the names of individuals who may transact business in the company's name.
corporate bond	A legally binding obligation of a corporation to repay a principal amount of debt along with interest at a predetermined rate and schedule.
corporation	A perpetual entity that survives after the death of its officers, directors, and stockholders. It is the most common form of business entity.
correspondent broker dealer	A broker dealer who introduces customer accounts to a clearing broker dealer.
cost basis	The cost of an asset, including any acquisition costs. It is used to determine capital gains and losses.
cost depletion	A method used to determine the tax deductions for investors in oil and gas programs.
cost of carry	All costs incurred by an investor for maintaining a position in a security, including margin interest and opportunity costs.
coterminous	Municipalities that share the same borders and have overlapping debt.
coupon bond	*See* bearer bond.
coupon yield	*See* nominal yield.
covenant	A promise made by an issuer of debt that describes the issuer's obligations and the bondholders' rights.

covered call	The sale of a call against a long position in the underlying security.
covered put	The sale of a put against a short position in the underlying security or against cash that will allow the person to purchase the security if the put is exercised.
CPI	*See* consumer price index (CPI).
credit agreement	The portion of the margin agreement that describes the terms and conditions under which credit will be extended to the customer.
credit balance	The cash balance in a customer's account.
credit department	*See* margin department.
credit risk	The risk that the issuer of debt securities will default on its obligation to pay interest or principal on a timely basis.
credit spread	An option position that results in a net premium or credit received by the investor from the simultaneous purchase and sale of two calls or two puts on the same security.
crossed market	A market condition that results when a broker enters a bid for a stock that exceeds the offering price for that stock. Also a condition that may result when a broker enters an offer that is lower than the bid price for that stock.
crossing stock	The pairing off of two offsetting customer orders by the same floor broker. The floor broker executing the cross must first show the order to the crowd for possible price improvement before crossing the orders.
crossover point	The point at which all tax credits have been used up by a limited partnership; results in a tax liability for the partners.
cum rights	A stock that is the subject of a rights offering and is trading with the rights attached to the common stock.
cumulative preferred stock	A preferred stock that entitles the holder to receive unpaid dividends prior to the payment of any dividends to common stockholders. Dividends that accumulate in arrears on cumulative issues are always the first dividends to be paid by a corporation.
cumulative voting	A method of voting that allows stockholders to cast all of their votes for one director or to distribute them among the candidates they wish to vote for. Cumulative voting favors smaller investors by allowing them to have a larger say in the election of the board of directors.
current assets	Cash, securities, accounts receivable, and other assets that can be converted into cash within 12 months.
current liabilities	Corporate obligations, including accounts payable, that must be paid within 12 months.

current market value (CMV)/current market price (CMP)	The present value of a marketable security or of a portfolio of marketable securities.
current ratio	A measure of a corporation's short-term liquidity found by dividing its current assets by its current liabilities.
current yield	A relationship between a securities annual income relative to its current market price. Determined by dividing annual income by the current market price.
CUSIP (Committee on Uniform Securities Identification Procedures)	A committee that assigns identification numbers to securities to help identify them.
custodial account	An account operated by a custodian for the benefit of a minor.
custodian	A party responsible for managing an account for another party. In acting as a custodian, the individual or corporation must adhere to the prudent man rule and only take such actions as a prudent person would do for him- or herself.
customer	Any individual or entity that maintains an account with a broker dealer.
customer agreement	An agreement signed by a customer at the time the account is opened, detailing the conditions of the customer's relationship with the firm. The customer agreement usually contains a predispute arbitration clause.
customer ledger	A ledger that lists all customer cash and margin accounts.
customer protection rule	Rule 15C3-3 requires that customer assets be kept segregated from the firm assets.
cyclical industry	An industry whose prospects fluctuate with the business cycle.

D

Daily Bond Buyer	A daily publication for the municipal securities industry that publishes information related to the municipal bond market and official notices of sales.
dated date	The day when interest starts to accrue for bonds.
dealer	(1) A person or firm who transacts securities business for its own account. (2) A brokerage firm acting as a principal when executing a customer's transaction or making markets over the counter.
dealer paper	Commercial paper sold to the public by a dealer, rather than placed with investors directly by the issuer.
debenture	An unsecured promissory note issued by a corporation backed only by the issuer's credit and promise to pay.

debit balance	The amount of money a customer owes a broker dealer.
debit spread	An option position that results in a net premium paid by the investor from the simultaneous purchase and sale of two calls or two puts on the same security.
debt securities	A security that represents a loan to the issuer. The owner of a debt security is a creditor of the issuing entity, be it a corporation or a government.
debt service	The scheduled interest payments and repayment of principal for debt securities.
debt service account	An account set up by a municipal issuer to pay the debt service of municipal revenue bonds.
debt service ratio	Indicates the issuer's ability to pay its interest and principal payments.
debt-to-equity ratio	A ratio that shows how highly leveraged the company is. It is found by dividing total long-term debt by total shareholder equity.
declaration date	The day chosen by the board of directors of a corporation to pay a dividend to shareholders.
deduction	An adjustment taken from gross income to reduce tax liability.
default	The failure of an issuer of debt securities to make interest and principal payments when they are due.
default risk	*See* credit risk.
defeasance	Results in the elimination of the issuer's debt obligations by issuing a new debt instrument to pay off the outstanding issue. The old issue is removed from the issuer's balance sheet and the proceeds of the new issue are placed in an escrow account to pay off the now-defeased issue.
defensive industry	A term used to describe a business whose economic prospects are independent from the business cycle. Pharmaceutical companies, utilities, and food producers are examples of defensive industries.
deferred annuity	A contract between an individual and an insurance company that delays payments to the annuitant until some future date.
deferred compensation plan	A contractual agreement between an employer and an employee under which the employee elects to defer receiving money owed until after retirement. Deferred compensation plans are typically unfunded, and the employee could lose all the money due under the agreement if the company goes out of business.
deficiency letter	A letter sent to a corporate issuer by the SEC, requesting additional information regarding the issuer's registration statement.
defined benefit plan	A qualified retirement plan established to provide a specific amount of retirement income for the plan participants. Unlike a defined contribution plan, the individual's retirement benefits are known prior to reaching retirement.

defined contribution plan	A qualified retirement plan that details the amount of money that the employer will contribute to the plan for the benefit of the employee. This amount is usually expressed as a percentage of the employee's gross annual income. The actual retirement benefits are not known until the employee reaches retirement, and the amount of the retirement benefit is a result of the contributions to the plan, along with the investment experience of the plan.
deflation	The economic condition that is characterized by a persistent decline in overall prices.
delivery	As used in the settlement process, results in the change of ownership of cash or securities.
delivery vs. payment	A type of settlement option that requires that the securities be physically received at the time payment is made.
delta	A measure of an option's price change in relation to a price change in the underlying security.
demand deposit	A deposit that a customer has with a bank or other financial institution that will allow the customer to withdraw the money at any time or on demand.
Department of Enforcement	The FINRA committee that has original jurisdiction over complaints and violations.
depletion	A tax deduction taken for the reduction in the amount of natural resources (e.g., gas, gold, oil) available to a business or partnership.
depreciation	A tax deduction taken for the reduction of value in a capital asset.
depreciation expense	A noncash expense that results in a reduction in taxable income.
depression	An economic condition that is characterized by a protracted decline in economic output and a rising level of unemployment.
derivative	A security that derives its value in whole or in part based on the price of another security. Options and futures are examples of derivative securities.
designated order	An order entered by an institution for a new issue of municipal bonds that states what firm and what agent is going to get the sales credit for the order.
devaluation	A significant fall in the value of a country's currency relative to other currencies. Devaluation could be the result of poor economic prospects in the home country. In extreme circumstances, it can be the result of government intervention.
developmental drilling program	An oil or gas program that drills for wells in areas of proven reserves.
developmental fee	A fee paid to organizers of a direct participation plan for the development of plans, obtaining financing or zoning authorizations, and other services.

diagonal spread	A spread that is created through the simultaneous purchase and sale of two calls or two puts on the same underlying security that differ in both strike price and expiration months.
dilution	A reduction in a stockholder's proportional ownership of a corporation as a result of the issuance of more shares. Earnings per share may also be diluted as a result of the issuance of additional shares.
direct debt	The total amount of a municipality's debt that has been issued by the municipality for its own benefit and for which the municipality is responsible to repay.
direct paper	Commercial paper sold to investors directly from the issuer without the use of a dealer.
direct participation program (DPP)	An entity that allows all taxable events to be passed through to investors, including limited partnerships and subchapter S corporations.
discount	The amount by which the price of a security is lower than its par value.
discount bond	A bond that is selling for a price that is lower than its par value.
discount rate	The rate that is charged to Federal Reserve member banks on loans directly from the Federal Reserve. This rate is largely symbolic, and member banks only borrow directly from the Federal Reserve as a last resort.
discretion	Authorization given to a firm or a representative to determine which securities are to be purchased and sold for the benefit of the customer without the customer's prior knowledge or approval.
discretionary account	An account where the owner has given the firm or the representative authority to transact business without the customer's prior knowledge or approval. All discretionary accounts must be approved and monitored closely by a principal of the firm.
disintermediation	The flow of money from traditional bank accounts to alternative higher yielding investments. This is more likely to occur as the Federal Reserve tightens monetary policy and interest rates rise.
disposable income	The sum of money an individual has left after paying taxes and required expenditures.
disproportional allocation	A method used by FINRA to determine if a free-riding violation has occurred with respect to a hot issuer. A firm is only allowed to sell up to 10% of a new issue to conditionally approved purchasers.
disproportionate sharing	An oil and gas sharing arrangement where the general partner pays a portion of the cost but receives a larger portion of the program's revenues.
distribution	Cash or property sent to shareholders or partners.

distribution stage	The period of time during which an annuitant is receiving payments from an annuity contract.
diversification	The distribution of investment capital among different investment choices. By purchasing several different investments, investors may be able to reduce their overall risk by minimizing the impact of any one security's adverse performance.
diversified fund/ diversified management company	A mutual fund that distributes its investment capital among a wide variety of investments. In order for a mutual fund to market itself as a diversified mutual fund it must meet the 75-5-10 rule: 75% of the fund's assets must be invested in securities issued by other entities, no more than 5% of the fund's assets may be invested in any one issuer, and the fund may own no more than 10% of any one company's outstanding securities.
dividend	A distribution of corporate assets to shareholders. A dividend may be paid in cash, stock, or property or product.
dividend department	The department in a brokerage firm that is responsible for the collecting of dividends and crediting them to customer accounts.
dividend disbursement agent	An agent of the issuer who pays out the dividends to shareholders of record.
dividend payout ratio	The amount of a company's earnings that were paid out to shareholders relative to the total earnings that were available to be paid out to shareholders. It can be calculated by dividing dividends per share by earnings per share.
dividend yield	Also known as a stock's current yield. It is a relationship between the annual dividends paid to shareholders relative to the stock's current market price. To determine a stock's dividend yield, divide annual dividends by the current market price.
DJIA	*See* Dow Jones Industrial Average.
doctrine of mutual reciprocity	An agreement that the federal government would not tax interest income received by investors in municipal bonds and that reciprocally the states would not tax interest income received by investors in federal debt obligations.
dollar bonds	A term issue of municipal bonds that are quoted as a percentage of par rather than on a yield basis.
dollar-cost averaging	A strategy of investing a fixed sum of money on a regular basis into a fluctuating market price. Over time an investor should be able to achieve an average cost per share that is below the average price per share. Dollar-cost averaging is a popular investment strategy with mutual fund investors.
donor	A person who gives a gift of cash or securities to another person. Once the gift has been made, the donor no longer has any rights or claim to the security. All gifts to a minor are irrevocable.

do not reduce (DNR)	An order qualifier for an order placed under the market that stipulates that the price of the order is not to be reduced for the distribution of ordinary dividends.
don't know (DK)	A term used to describe a dealer's response to a confirmation for a trade they "don't know" doing.
Dow Jones Composite Average	An index composed of 65 stocks that is used as an indicator of market performance.
Dow Jones Industrial Average (DJIA)	An index composed of 30 industrial companies. The Dow Jones is the most widely quoted market index.
Dow Jones Transportation Average	An index composed of 20 transportation stocks.
Dow Jones Utility Average	An index composed of 15 utility stocks.
Dow theory	A theory that believes that the health both of the market and of the economy may be predicted by the performance of the Dow Jones Industrial Average.
dry hole	A term used to describe a nonproducing well.
dual-purpose fund	A mutual fund that offers two classes of shares to investors. One class is sold to investors seeking income and the other class is sold to investors seeking capital appreciation.

E

early withdrawal penalty	A penalty tax charged to an investor for withdrawing money from a qualified retirement plan prior to age 59-1/2, usually 10% on top of ordinary income taxes.
earned income	Money received by an individual in return for performing services.
earnings per share	The net amount of a corporation's earnings available to common shareholders divided by the number of common shares outstanding.
earnings per share fully diluted	The net amount of a corporation's earnings available to common shareholders after taking into consideration the potential conversion of all convertible securities.
eastern account	A type of syndicate account that requires all members to be responsible for their own allocation as well as for their proportional share of any member's unsold securities.
economic risk	The risk of loss of principal associated with the purchase of securities.
EE savings bonds	Nonmarketable U.S. government zero-coupon bonds that must be purchased from the government and redeemed to the government.

effective date	The day when a new issue's registration with the SEC becomes effective. Once the issue's registration statement has become effective, the securities may then be sold to investors.
efficient market theory	A theory that states that the market operates and processes information efficiently and prices in all information as soon as it becomes known.
Employee Retirement Income Security Act of 1974 (ERISA)	The legislation that governs the operation of private-sector pension plans. Corporate pension plans organized under ERISA guidelines qualify for beneficial tax treatment by the IRS.
endorsement	The signature on the back of a security that allows its ownership to be transferred.
EPS	*See* earnings per share.
equipment leasing limited partnership	A limited partnership that is organized to purchase equipment and lease it to corporations to earn lease income and to shelter passive income for investors.
equipment trust certificate	A bond backed by a pledge of large equipment, such as airplanes, railroad cars, and ships.
equity	A security that represents the ownership in a corporation. Both preferred and common equity holders have an ownership interest in the corporation.
equity financing	The sale of common or preferred equity by a corporation in an effort to raise capital.
equity option	An option to purchase or sell common stock.
ERISA	*See* Employee Retirement Income Security Act of 1974.
erroneous report	A report of an execution given in error to a client. The report is not binding on the firm or on the agent.
escrow agreement	Evidence of ownership of a security provided to a broker dealer as proof of ownership of the underlying security for covered call writers.
Eurobond	A bond issued in domestic currency of the issuer but sold outside of the issuer's country.
Eurodollar	A deposit held outside of the United States denominated in U.S. dollars.
Eurodollar bonds	A bond issued by a foreign issuer denominated in U.S. dollars.
Euroyen bonds	Bonds issued outside of Japan but denominated in yen.
excess equity (EE)	The value of an account's equity in excess of Regulation T.
exchange	A market, whether physical or electronic, that provides a forum for trading securities through a dual-auction process.
exchange distribution	A distribution of a large block of stock on the floor of the exchange that is crossed with offsetting orders.

exchange privilege	The right offered by many mutual funds that allows an investor to transfer or move money between different portfolios offered through the same fund company. An investor may redeem shares of the fund, which is being sold at the NAV, and purchase shares of the new portfolio at the NAV without paying another sales charge.
ex date/ex-dividend date	The first day when purchasers of a security will no longer be entitled to receive a previously declared dividend.
executor/executrix	An individual with the authority to manage the affairs of a decedent's estate.
exempt security	A security that is exempt from the registration requirements of the Securities Act of 1933.
exempt transaction	A transaction that is not subject to state registration.
exercise	An investor's election to take advantage of the rights offered through the terms of an option, a right, or a warrant.
exercise price	The price at which an option investor may purchase or sell a security. Also the price at which an investor may purchase a security through a warrant or right.
existing property program	A type of real estate direct participation program that purchases existing property for the established rental income.
expansion	A period marked by a general increase in business activity and an increase in gross domestic product.
expansionary policy	A monetary policy enacted through the Federal Reserve Board that increases money supply and reduces interest rates in an effort to stimulate the economy.
expense ratio	The amount of a mutual fund's expenses relative to its assets. The higher the expense ratio, the lower the investor's return. A mutual fund's expense ratio tells an investor how efficiently a mutual fund operates, not how profitable the mutual fund is.
expiration cycle	A 4-month cycle for option expiration: January, April, July, and October; February, May, August, and November; or March, June, September, and December.
expiration date	The date on which an option ceases to exist.
exploratory drilling program	A direct participation program that engages in the drilling for oil or gas in new areas seeking to find new wells.
exploratory well	Also known as wildcatting. The drilling for oil or gas in new areas in an effort to find new wells.
ex rights	The common stock subject to a rights offering trade without the rights attached.

ex rights date	The first day when the common stock is subject to a rights offering trade without the rights attached.
ex warrants	Common trading without the warrants attached.

F

face-amount certificate company (FAC)	A type of investment company that requires an investor to make fixed payments over time or to deposit a lump sum, and that will return to the investor a stated sum known as the face amount on a specific date.
face amount/face value	*See* par.
fail to deliver	An event where the broker on the sell side of the transaction fails to deliver the security.
fail to receive	An event where the broker on the buy side of the transaction fails to receive the security from the broker on the sell side.
Fannie Mae	*See* Federal National Mortgage Association.
Farm Credit Administrator	The agency that oversees all of the activities of the banks in the Federal Farm Credit System.
Federal Deposit Insurance Corporation (FDIC)	The government insurance agency that provides insurance for bank depositors in case of bank failure.
Federal Farm Credit System	An organization of banks that is designed to provide financing to farmers for mortgages, feed and grain, and equipment.
federal funds rate	The rate banks charge each other on overnight loans.
Federal Home Loan Mortgage Corporation (FHLMC; Freddie Mac)	A publicly traded for-profit corporation that provides liquidity to the secondary mortgage market by purchasing pools of mortgages from lenders and, in turn, issues mortgage-backed securities.
Federal Intermediate Credit Bank	Provides short-term financing to farmers for equipment.
Federal National Mortgage Association (FNMA; Fannie Mae)	A publicly traded for-profit corporation that provides liquidity to the secondary mortgage market by purchasing pools of mortgages and issuing mortgage-backed securities.
Federal Open Market Committee (FOMC)	The committee of the Federal Reserve Board that makes policy decisions relating to the nation's money supply.

Federal Reserve Board	A seven-member board that directs the policies of the Federal Reserve System. The members are appointed by the President and approved by Congress.
Federal Reserve System	The nation's central banking system, the purpose of which is to regulate money supply and the extension of credit. The Federal Reserve System is composed of 12 central banks and 24 regional banks, along with hundreds of national and state chartered banks.
fictitious quote	A quote that is not representative of an actual bid or offer for a security.
fidelity bond	A bond that must be posted by all broker dealers to ensure the public against employee dishonesty.
fill or kill (FK)	A type of order that requires that all of the securities in the order be purchased or sold immediately or not at all.
final prospectus	The official offering document for a security that contains the security's final offering price along with all information required by law for an investor to make an informed decision.
firm commitment underwriting	Guarantees the issuer all of the money right away. The underwriters purchase all of the securities from the issuer regardless of whether they can sell the securities to their customers.
firm quote	A quote displayed at which the dealer is obligated to buy or sell at least one round lot at the quoted price.
fiscal policy	Government policy designed to influence the economy through government tax and spending programs. The President and Congress control fiscal policy.
5% markup policy	FINRA's guideline that requires all prices paid by customers to be reasonably related to a security's market price. The 5% policy is a guideline, not a rule, and it does not apply to securities sold through a prospectus.
fixed annuity	An insurance contract where the insurance company guarantees fixed payments to the annuitant, usually until the annuitant's death.
fixed assets	Assets used by a corporation to conduct its business, such as plant and equipment.
flat	A term used to describe a bond that trades without accrued interest, such as a zero-coupon bond or a bond that is in default.
floor broker	An individual member of an exchange who may execute orders on the floor.
floor trader	Members of the exchange who trade for their own accounts. Members of the NYSE may not trade from the floor for their own accounts.
flow of funds	A schedule of expenses and interested parties that prioritizes how payments will be made from the revenue generated by a facility financed by a municipal revenue bond.

forced conversion	The calling in of convertible bonds at a price that is less than the market value of the underlying common stock into which the bonds may be converted.
foreign currency	Currency of another country.
foreign currency option	An option to purchase or sell a specified amount of another country's currency.
Form 10-K	An annual report filed by a corporation detailing its financial performance for the year.
Form 10-Q	A quarterly report filed by a corporation detailing its financial performance for the quarter.
form letter	A letter sent out by a brokerage firm or a registered representative to more than 25 people in a 90-day period. Form letters are subject to approval and recordkeeping requirements.
forward pricing	The way in which open-end mutual funds are valued for investors who wish to purchase or redeem shares of the fund. Mutual funds usually price their shares at the end of the business day. The price to be paid or received by the investor will be the price that is next calculated after the fund receives the order.
401K	A qualified retirement plan offered by an employer.
403B	A qualified retirement plan offered to teachers and employees of nonprofit organizations.
fourth market	A transaction between two large institutions without the use of a broker dealer.
fractional share	A portion of a whole share that represents ownership of an open-end mutual fund.
fraud	Any attempt to gain an unfair advantage over another party through the use of deception, concealment, or misrepresentation.
free credit balance	Cash reserves in a customer's account that have not been invested. Customers must be notified of their free credit balances at least quarterly.
free look	A privilege offered to purchasers of contractual plans and insurance policies that will allow the individual to cancel the contract within the free-look period, usually 45 days.
freeriding	The purchase and sale of a security without depositing the money required to cover the purchase price as required by Regulation T.
freeriding and withholding	The withholding of new issue securities offered by a broker dealer for the benefit of the brokerage firm or an employee.
front-end load	(1) A sales charge paid by investors in open-end mutual funds that is paid at the time of purchase. (2) A contractual plan that seeks to assess sales

charges in the first years of the plan and may charge up to 50% of the first year's payments as sales charges.

frozen account   An account where the owner is required to deposit cash or securities up front, prior to any purchase or sale taking place. An account is usually frozen as a result of a customer's failure to pay or deliver securities.

full power of attorney   A type of discretionary authority that allows a third party to purchase and sell securities as well as to withdraw cash and securities without the owner's prior consent or knowledge. This type of authority is usually reserved to trustees and attorneys.

fully registered bonds   A type of bond issuance where the issuer has a complete record of the owners of the bonds and who is entitled to receive interest and principal payments. The owners of fully registered bonds are not required to clip coupons.

functional allocation   An arrangement for oil and gas programs where the general partner pays the tangible drilling costs and the limited partner absorbs the intangible drilling costs.

fundamental analyst   A method of valuing the company that takes into consideration the financial performance of the corporation, the value of its assets, and the quality of its management.

funded debt   Long-term debt obligations of corporations or municipalities.

fungible   Easily exchangeable items with the same conditions.

G

general account   An insurance company's account that holds the money and investments for fixed contracts and traditional life insurance policies.

general obligation bond   A municipal bond that is backed by the taxing power of the state or municipality.

general partner   The partner in a general partnership who manages the business and is responsible for any debt of the program.

general securities principal   An individual who has passed the Series 24 exam and may supervise the activities of the firm and its agents.

generic advertising   Advertising designed to promote name recognition for a firm and securities as investments, but does not recommend specific securities.

good 'til cancel (GTC)   An order that remains on the books until it is executed or canceled.

goodwill   An intangible asset of a corporation, such as its name recognition and reputation, that adds to its value.

Government National Mortgage Association (GNMA; Ginnie Mae)	A government corporation that provides liquidity to the mortgage markets by purchasing pools of mortgages that have been insured by the Federal Housing Administration and the Veterans Administration. Ginnie Mae issues pass-through certificates to investors backed by the pools of mortgages.
government security	A security that is an obligation of the U.S. government and that is backed by the full faith and credit of the U.S. government, such as Treasury bills, notes, and bonds.
grant anticipation note (GAN)	Short-term municipal financing issued in anticipation of receiving a grant from the federal government or one of its agencies.
greenshoe option	An option given to an underwriter of common stock that will allow it to purchase up to an additional 15% of the offering from the issuer at the original offering price to cover over-allotments for securities that are in high demand.
gross domestic product (GDP)	The value of all goods and services produced by a country within a period of time. GDP includes government purchases, investments, and exports minus imports.
gross income	All income received by a taxpayer before deductions for taxes.
gross revenue pledge	A flow-of-funds pledge for a municipal revenue bond that states that debt service will be paid first.
growth fund	A fund whose objective is capital appreciation. Growth funds invest in common stocks to achieve their objective.
growth stock	The stock of a company whose earnings grow at a rate that is faster than the growth rate of the economy as a whole. Growth stocks are characterized by increased opportunities for appreciation and little or no dividends.
guardian	An individual who has a fiduciary responsibility for another, usually a minor.

H

halt	A temporary stop in the trading of a security. If a common stock is halted, all derivatives and convertibles will be halted as well.
head and shoulders	A chart pattern that indicates a reversal of a trend. A head-and-shoulders top indicates a reversal of an uptrend and is considered bearish. A head-and-shoulders bottom is the reversal of a downtrend and is considered bullish.
hedge	A position taken in a security to offset or reduce the risk associated with the risk of another security.

HH bond	A nonmarketable government security that pays semiannual interest. Series HH bonds are issued with a $500 minimum value and may only be purchased by trading matured series EE bonds; they may not be purchased with cash.
high	The highest price paid for a security during a trading session or during a 52-week period.
holder	An individual or corporation that owns a security. The holder of a security is also known as being long the security.
holding period	The length of time during which an investor owns a security. The holding period is important for calculating tax liability.
hold in street name	The registration of customer securities in the name of the broker dealer. Most customers register securities in the name of the broker dealer to make the transfer of ownership easier.
horizontal spread	Also known as a calendar spread. The simultaneous purchase and sale of two calls or two puts on the same underlying security with the same exercise price but with different expiration months.
hot issue	A new issue of securities that trades at an immediate premium to its offering price in the secondary market.
HR 10 plan	*See* Keogh plan.
hypothecation	The customer's pledge of securities as collateral for a margin loan.

I

immediate annuity	An annuity contract purchased with a single payment that entitles the holder to receive immediate payments from the contract. The annuitant purchases annuity units and usually begins receiving payments within 60 days.
immediate family	An individual's immediate family includes parents, parents-in-law, children, spouse, and any relative financially dependent upon the individual.
immediate or cancel (IOC)	An order that is to be executed as fully as possible immediately and whatever is not executed will be canceled.
income bond	A highly speculative bond that is issued at a discount from par and only pays interest if the issuer has enough income to do so. The issuer of the income bond only promises to pay principal at maturity. Income bonds trade flat without accrued interest.
income fund	A mutual fund whose investment objective is to achieve current income for its shareholders by investing in bonds and preferred stocks.
income program	A type of oil and gas program that purchases producing wells to receive the income received from the sale of the proven reserves.

income statement	A financial statement that shows a corporation's revenue and expenses for the time period in question.
indefeasible title	A record of ownership that cannot be challenged.
index	A representation of the price action of a given group of securities. Indexes are used to measure the condition of the market as a whole, such as with the S&P 500, or can be used to measure the condition of an industry group, such as with the Biotech index.
index option	An option on an underlying financial index. Index options settle in cash.
indication of interest	An investor's expression of a willingness to purchase a new issue of securities after receiving a preliminary prospectus. The investor's indication of interest is not binding on either the investor or the firm.
Individual Retirement Account (IRA)	A self-directed retirement account that allows individuals with earned income to contribute the lesser of 100% of earned income or the annual maximum per year. The contributions may be made with pre- or after-tax dollars, depending on the individual's level of income and whether he or she is eligible to participate in an employer's sponsored plan.
industrial development bond	A private-purpose municipal bond whose proceeds are used to build a facility that is leased to a corporation. The debt service on the bonds is supported by the lease payments.
inflation	The persistent upward pressure on the price of goods and services over time.
initial margin requirement	The initial amount of equity that a customer must deposit to establish a position. The initial margin requirement is set by the Federal Reserve Board under Regulation T.
initial public offering (IPO)	The first offering of common stock to the general investing public.
in part call	A partial call of a bond issue for redemption.
inside information	Information that is not known to people outside of the corporation. Information becomes public only after it is released by the corporation through a recognized media source. Inside information may be both material and immaterial. It is only illegal to trade on inside material information.
inside market	The highest bid and the lowest offer for a security.
insider	A company's officers, directors, large stockholders of 10% or more of the company, and anyone who is in possession of nonpublic material information, along with the immediate family members of the same.

Insider Trading and Securities Fraud Enforcement Act of 1988	Federal legislation that made the penalties for people trading on material nonpublic information more severe. Penalties for insider traders are up to the greater of 300% of the amount of money made or the loss avoided or $1 million and up to 5 years in prison. People who disseminate inside information may be imprisoned and fined up to $1 million.
INSTINET	A computer network that facilitates trading of large blocks of stocks between institutions without the use of a broker dealer.
institutional account	An account in the name of an institution but operated for the benefit of others (i.e., banks and mutual funds). There is no minimum size for an institutional account.
institutional communication	Any communication that is distributed exclusively to institutional investors. Institutional communication does not require the preapproval of a principal but must be maintained for 3 years by the firm.
institutional investor	An investor who trades for its own account or for the accounts of others in large quantities and is covered by fewer protective laws.
insurance covenant	The promise of an issuer of revenue bonds to maintain insurance on the financed project.
intangible asset	Nonphysical property of a corporation, such as trademarks and copyrights.
intangible drilling cost (IDC)	Costs for an oil and gas program that are expensed in the year in which they are incurred for such things as wages, surveys, and well casings.
interbank market	An international currency market.
interest	The cost for borrowing money, usually charged at an annual percentage rate.
interest rate option	An option based on U.S. government securities. The options are either rate-based or priced-based options.
interest rate risk	The risk borne by investors in interest-bearing securities, which subjects the holder to a loss of principal should interest rates rise.
interlocking directorate	Corporate boards that share one or more directors.
Intermarket Trading System/ Computer-Assisted Execution System (ITS/CAES)	A computer system that links the third market for securities with the exchanges.
Internal Revenue Code (IRC)	The codes that define tax liabilities for U.S. taxpayers.

interpositioning	The placing of another broker dealer in between the customer and the best market. Interpositioning is prohibited unless it can be demonstrated that the customer received a better price because of it.
interstate offering	A multistate offering of securities that requires that the issuer register with the SEC as well as with the states in which the securities will be sold.
in the money	A relationship between the strike price of an option and the underlying security's price. A call is in the money when the strike price is lower than the security's price. A put is in the money when the strike price is higher than the security's price.
intrastate offering	*See* Rule 147.
intrinsic value	The amount by which an option is in the money.
introducing broker	*See* correspondent broker dealer.
inverted yield curve	A yield curve where the cost of short-term financing exceeds the cost of long-term financing.
investment adviser	Anyone who charges a fee for investment advice or who holds himself out to the public as being in the business of giving investment advice for a fee.
Investment Advisers Act of 1940	The federal legislation that sets forth guidelines for business requirements and activities of investment advisers.
investment banker	A financial institution that is in the business of raising capital for companies and municipalities by underwriting securities.
investment company	A company that sells undivided interests in a pool of securities and manages the portfolio for the benefit of the investors. Investment companies include management companies, unit investment trusts, and face-amount companies.
Investment Company Act of 1940	Federal legislation that regulates the operation and registration of investment companies.
investment-grade security	A security that has been assigned a rating in the highest rating tier by a recognized ratings agency.
investment objective	An investor's set of goals as to how he or she is seeking to make money, such as capital appreciation or current income.
investor	The purchaser of a security who seeks to realize a profit.
IRA rollover	The temporary distribution of assets from an IRA and the subsequent reinvestment of the assets into another IRA within 60 days. An IRA may be rolled over only once per year and is subject to a 10% penalty and ordinary income taxes if the investor is under 59-1/2 and if the assets are not deposited in another qualified account within 60 days.

IRA transfer	The movement of assets from one qualified account to another without the account holder taking possession of the assets. Investors may transfer an IRA as often as they like.
issued stock	Stock that has actually been sold to the investing public.
issuer	Any entity that issues or proposes to issue securities.

J

joint account	An account that is owned by two or more parties. Joint accounts allow either party to enter transactions for the account. Both parties must sign a joint account agreement. All joint accounts must be designated as joint tenants in common or with rights of survivorship.
joint tenants in common (JTIC)	A joint account where the assets of a party who has died transfer to the decedent's estate, not the other tenant.
joint tenants with rights of survivorship (JTWROS)	A joint account where the assets of a party who has died transfer to the surviving party, not the decedent's estate.
joint venture	An interest in an operation shared by two or more parties. The parties have no other relationship beyond the joint venture.
junk bond	A bond with a high degree of default risk that has been assigned a speculative rating by the ratings agencies.
junk bond fund	A speculative bond fund that invests in high-yield bonds in order to achieve a high degree of current income.

K

Keogh plan	A qualified retirement account for self-employed individuals. Contributions are limited to the lesser of 20% of their gross income or $51,000.
Keynesian economics	An economic theory that states that government intervention in the marketplace helps sustain economic growth.
know-your-customer rule	Industry regulation that requires a registered representative to be familiar with the customer's financial objectives and needs prior to making a recommendation; also known as Rule 405.

L

lagging indicator	A measurement of economic activity that changes after a change has taken place in economic activity. Lagging indicators are useful confirmation tools when determining the strength of an economic trend. Lagging indicators include corporate profits, average duration of unemployment, and labor costs.
last in, first out (LIFO)	An accounting method used that states that the last item that was produced is the first item sold.
leading indicator	A measurement of economic activity that changes prior to a change in economic activity. Leading economic indicators are useful in predicting a coming trend in economic activity. Leading economic indicators include housing permits, new orders for durable goods, and the S&P 500.
LEAPS (long-term equity anticipation securities)	A long-term option on a security that has an expiration of up to 39 months.
lease rental bonds	A municipal bond that is issued to finance the building of a facility that will be rented out. The lease payments on the facility will support the bond's debt service.
legal list	A list of securities that have been approved by certain state securities regulators for purchase by fiduciaries.
legal opinion	An opinion issued by a bond attorney stating that the issue is a legally binding obligation of the state or municipality. The legal opinion also contains a statement regarding the tax status of the interest payments received by investors.
legislative risk	The risk that the government may do something that adversely affects an investment.
letter of intent (LOI)	A letter signed by the purchaser of mutual fund shares that states the investor's intention to invest a certain amount of money over a 13-month period. By agreeing to invest this sum, the investor is entitled to receive a lower sales charge on all purchases covered by the letter of intent. The letter of intent may be backdated up to 90 days from an initial purchase. Should the investor fail to invest the stated sum, a sales charge adjustment will be charged.
level load	A mutual fund share that charges a flat annual fee, such as a 12B-1 fee.
level one	A Nasdaq workstation service that allows the agent to see the inside market only.
level two	A Nasdaq workstation service that allows the order-entry firm to see the inside market, to view the quotes entered by all market makers, and to execute orders.

level three	A Nasdaq workstation service that allows market-making firms to see the inside market, to view the quotes entered by all market makers, to execute orders, and to enter their own quotes for the security. This is the highest level of Nasdaq service.
leverage	The use of borrowed funds to try to obtain a rate of return that exceeds the cost of the funds.
liability	A legal obligation to pay a debt either incurred through borrowing or through the normal course of business.
life annuity/straight life	An annuity payout option that provides payments over the life of the annuitant.
life annuity with period certain	An annuity payout option that provides payments to the annuitant for life or to the annuitant's estate for the period certain, whichever is longer.
life contingency	An annuity payout option that provides a death benefit in case the annuitant dies during the accumulation stage.
limit order	An order that sets a maximum price that the investor will pay in the case of a buy order or the minimum price the investor will accept in the case of a sell order.
limited liability	A protection afforded to investors in securities that limits their liability to the amount of money invested in the securities.
limited partner	A passive investor in a direct participation program who has no role in the project's management.
limited partnership (LP)	An association of two or more partners with at least one partner being the general partner who is responsible for the management of the partnership.
limited partnership agreement	The foundation of all limited partnerships. The agreement is the contract between all partners, and it spells out the authority of the general partner and the rights of all limited partners.
limited power of attorney/limited trading authorization	Legal authorization for a representative or a firm to effect purchases and sales for a customer's account without the customer's prior knowledge. The authorization is limited to buying and selling securities and may not be given to another party.
limited principal	An individual who has passed the Series 26 exam and may supervise Series 6 limited representatives.
limited representative	An individual who has passed the Series 6 exam and may represent a broker dealer in the sale of mutual fund shares and variable contracts.
limited tax bond	A type of general obligation bond that is issued by a municipality that may not increase its tax rate to pay the debt service of the issue.

liquidity	The ability of an investment to be readily converted into cash.
liquidity risk	The risk that an investor may not be able to sell a security when needed or that selling a security when needed will adversely affect the price.
listed option	A standardized option contract that is traded on an exchange.
listed security	A security that trades on one of the exchanges. Only securities that trade on an exchange are known as listed securities.
loan consent agreement	A portion of the margin agreement that allows the broker dealer to loan out the customer's securities to another customer who wishes to borrow them to sell the security short.
locked market	A market condition that results when the bid and the offer for a security are equal.
LOI	*See* letter of intent.
London Interbank Offered Rate (LIBOR)	The interbank rates for dollar-denominated deposits in England.
long	A term used to describe an investor who owns a security.
long market value	The total long market value of a customer's account.
long-term gain	A profit realized through the sale of a security at a price that is higher than its purchase price after a being held for more than 12 months.
long-term loss	A loss realized through the sale of a security at a price that is lower than its purchase price after being held for more than 12 months.
loss carry forward	A capital loss realized on the sale of an asset in 1 year that is carried forward in whole or part to subsequent tax years.
low	The lowest price at which a security has traded in any given period, usually measured during a trading day or for 52 weeks.

M

M1	The most liquid measure of the money supply. It includes all currency and demand and NOW deposits (checking accounts).
M2	A measure of the money supply that includes M1 plus all time deposits, savings accounts, and noninstitutional money market accounts.
M3	A measure of the money supply that includes M2 and large time deposits, institutional money market funds, short-term repurchase agreements, and other large liquid assets.

maintenance call	A demand for additional cash or collateral made by a broker dealer when a margin customer's account equity has fallen below the minimum requirement of the NYSE or that is set by the broker dealer.
maintenance covenant	A promise made by an issuer of a municipal revenue bond to maintain the facility in good repair.
Major Market Index (XMI)	An index created by the Amex to AMEX 15 of the 30 largest stocks in the Dow Jones Industrial Average.
Maloney Act of 1938	An amendment to the Securities Exchange Act of 1934 that gave the NASD (now part of FINRA) the authority to regulate the over-the-counter market.
managed underwriting	An underwriting conducted by a syndicate led by the managing underwriter.
management company	A type of investment company that actively manages a portfolio of securities in order to meet a stated investment objective. Management companies are also known as mutual funds.
management fee	(1) The fee received by the lead or managing underwriter of a syndicate. (2) The fee received by a sponsor of a direct participation program.
managing partner	The general partner in a direct participation program.
managing underwriter	The lead underwriter in a syndicate who is responsible for negotiating with the issuer, forming the syndicate, and settling the syndicate account.
margin	The amount of customer equity that is required to hold a position in a security.
margin account	An account that allows the customer to borrow money from the brokerage firm to buy securities.
margin call	A demand for cash or collateral mandated by the Federal Reserve Board under Regulation T.
margin department	The department in a broker dealer that calculates money owed by the customer or money due the customer.
margin maintenance call	*See* maintenance call.
mark to the market	The monitoring of a the current value of a position relative to the price at which the trade was executed for securities purchased on margin or on a when-issued basis.
markdown	The profit earned by a dealer on a transaction when purchasing securities for its own account from a customer.
marketability	The ability of an investment to be exchanged between two investors. A security with an active secondary market has a higher level of marketability than one whose market is not as active.

market arbitrage	A type of arbitrage that consists of purchasing a security in one marketplace and selling it in another to take advantage of price inefficiencies.
market letter	A regular publication, usually issued by an investment adviser, that offers information and/or advice regarding a security, market conditions, or the economy as a whole.
market maker	A Nasdaq firm that is required to quote a continuous two-sided market for the securities in which it trades.
market not held	A type of order that gives the floor broker discretion over the time and price of execution.
market on close	An order that will be executed at whatever price the market is at, either on the closing print or just prior to the closing print.
market on open	An order that will be executed at whatever price the market is at, either on the opening print or just after the opening print.
market order	A type of order that will be executed immediately at the best available price once it is presented to the market.
market-out clause	A clause in an underwriting agreement that gives the syndicate the ability to cancel the underwriting if it finds a material problem with the information or condition of the issuer.
market risk/ systematic risk	The risk inherent in any investment in the market that states an investor may lose money simply because the market is going down.
market value	The value of a security that is determined in the marketplace by the investors who enter bids and offers for a security.
markup	The compensation paid to a securities dealer for selling a security to a customer from its inventory.
markup policy	FINRA's guideline that states that the price that is paid or received by an investor must be reasonably related to the market price for that security. FINRA offers 5% as a guideline for what is reasonable to charge investors when they purchase or sell securities.
material information	Information that would affect a company's current or future prospects or an investor's decision to invest in the company.
maturity date	The date on which a bond's principal amount becomes payable to its holders.
member	A member of FINRA or one of the 1,366 members of the NYSE.
member firm	A firm that is a member of the NYSE, FINRA, or another self-regulatory organization.
member order	A retail order entered by a member of a municipal bond syndicate for which the member will receive all of the sales credit.

mini maxi underwriting	A type of best efforts underwriting that states that the offering will not become effective until a minimum amount is sold and sets a maximum amount that may be sold.
minimum death benefit	The minimum guaranteed death benefit that will be paid to the beneficiaries if the holder of a variable life insurance policy dies.
minus tick	A trade in an exchange-listed security that is at a price that is lower than the previous trade.
modern portfolio theory	An investing approach that looks at the overall return and risk of a portfolio as a whole, not as a collection of single investments.
modified accelerated cost recovery system (MACRS)	An accounting method that allows the owner to recover a larger portion of the asset's value in the early years of its life.
monetarist theory	A theory that states that the money supply is the driving force in the economy and that a well-managed money supply will benefit the economy.
monetary policy	Economic policy that is controlled by the Federal Reserve Board and controls the amount of money in circulation and the level of interest rates.
money market	The secondary market where short-term highly liquid securities are traded. Securities traded in the money market include T-bills, negotiable CDs, bankers' acceptances, commercial paper, and other short-term securities with less than 12 months to maturity.
money market mutual fund	A mutual fund that invests in money market instruments to generate monthly interest for its shareholders. Money market mutual funds have a stable NAV that is equal to $1, but it is not guaranteed.
money supply	The total amount of currency, loans, and credit in the economy. The money supply is measured by M1, M2, M3, and L.
moral obligation bond	A type of municipal revenue bond that will allow the state or municipality to vote to cover a shortfall in the debt service.
multiplier effect	The ability of the money supply to grow simply through the normal course of banking. When banks and other financial institutions accept deposits and subsequently loan out those deposits to earn interest, the amount of money in the system grows.
municipal bond	A bond issued by a state or political subdivision of a state in an effort to finance its operations. Interest earned by investors in municipal bonds is almost always free from federal income taxes.
municipal bond fund	A mutual fund that invests in a portfolio of municipal debt in an effort to produce income that is free from federal income taxes for its investors.

Municipal Bond Investors Assurance Corp. (MBIA)	An independent insurance company that will, for a fee received from the issuer, insure the interest and principal payments on a municipal bond.
municipal note	A short-term municipal issue sold to manage the issuer's cash flow, usually in anticipation of the offering of long-term financing.
Municipal Securities Rulemaking Board (MSRB)	The self-regulatory organization that oversees the issuance and trading of municipal bonds. The MSRB's rules are enforced by other industry SROs.
Munifacts	A service that provides real-time secondary market quotes. Munifacts is now known as Thomson Muni Market Monitor.
mutual fund	An investment company that invests in and manages a portfolio of securities for its shareholders. Open-end mutual funds sell their shares to investors on a continuous basis and must stand ready to redeem their shares upon the shareholder's request.
mutual fund custodian	A qualified financial institution that maintains physical custody of a mutual fund's cash and securities. Custodians are usually banks, trust companies, or exchange member firms.

N

naked	The sale of a call option without owning the underlying security or the sale of a put option without being short the stock or having cash on deposit that is sufficient to purchase the underlying security.
narrow-based index	An index that is based on a market sector or a limited number of securities.
NASD (National Association of Securities Dealers)	The industry self-regulatory agency that was authorized by the Maloney Act of 1938 and empowered to regulate the over-the-counter market. The NASD is now part of FINRA.
NASD bylaws	The rules that define the operation of the NASD and how it regulates the over-the-counter market. The four major bylaws are the Rules of Fair Practice, the Uniform Practice Code, the Code of Procedure, and the Code of Arbitration. Now known as FINRA bylaws.
NASD Manual	An NASD publication that outlines the rules and regulations of NASD membership. Now known as the FINRA Manual.
National Securities Clearing Corporation (NSCC)	The clearing intermediary through which clearing member firms reconcile their securities accounts.

NAV (net asset value)	The net value of a mutual fund after deducting all its liabilities. A mutual fund must calculate its NAV at least once per business day. To determine NAV per share, simply divide the mutual fund's NAV by the total number of shares outstanding.
negotiability	The ability of an investment to be freely exchanged between noninterested parties.
negotiable certificate of deposit	A certificate issued by a bank for a time deposit in excess of $100,000 that can be exchanged between parties prior to its maturity date. FDIC insurance only covers the first $250,000 of the principal amount should the bank fail.
NOW (negotiable order of withdrawal) Account	A type of demand deposit that allows the holder to write checks against an interest-bearing account.
net change	The difference between the previous day's closing price and the price of the most recently reported trade for a security.
net current assets per share	A calculation of the value per share that excludes fixed assets and intangibles.
net debt per capita	A measure of a municipal issuer's ability to meet its obligations. It measures the debt level of the issuer in relation to the population.
net debt to assessed valuation	A measure of the issuer's ability to meet its obligations and to raise additional revenue through property taxes.
net direct debt	The total amount of general obligation debt, including notes and short-term financing, issued by a municipality or state.
net interest cost (NIC)	A calculation that measures the interest cost of a municipal issue over the life of all bonds. Most competitive underwritings for municipal securities are awarded to the syndicate that submits the bid with the lowest NIC.
net investment income	The total sum of investment income derived from dividend and interest income after subtracting expenses.
net revenue pledge	A pledge from a revenue bond that pays maintenance and operation expenses first, then debt service.
net total debt	The total of a municipality's direct debt plus its overlapping debt.
net worth	The value of a corporation after subtracting all of its liabilities. A corporation's net worth is also equal to shareholder's equity.
new account form	Paperwork that must be filled out and signed by the representative and a principal of the firm prior to the opening of any account being opened for a customer.

new construction program	A real estate program that seeks to achieve capital appreciation by building new properties.
new housing authority (NHA)	A municipal bond issued to build low-income housing. NHA bonds are guaranteed by the U.S. government and are considered the safest type of municipal bonds. NHA bonds are not considered to be double-barreled bonds.
new issue	*See* initial public offering (IPO).
New York Stock Exchange (NYSE)	A membership organization that provides a marketplace for securities to be exchanged in one centralized location through a dual-auction process.
no-load fund	A fund that does not charge the investor a sales charge to invest in the fund. Shares of no-load mutual funds are sold directly from the fund company to the investor.
nominal owner	An individual or entity registered as the owner of record of securities for the benefit of another party.
nominal quote	A quote given for informational purposes only. A trader who identifies a quote as being nominal cannot be held to trading at the prices that were clearly identified as being nominal.
nominal yield	The yield that is stated or named on the security. The nominal yield, once it has been set, never changes, regardless of the market price of the security.
noncompetitive bid	A bid submitted for Treasury bills where the purchaser agrees to accept the average of all yields accepted at the auction. Noncompetitive tenders are always the first orders filled at the auction.
noncumulative preferred	A type of preferred stock whose dividends do not accumulate in arrears if the issuer misses the payment.
nondiscrimination	A clause that states that all eligible individuals must be allowed to participate in a qualified retirement plan.
nondiversification	An investment strategy that concentrates its investments among a small group of securities or issuers.
nondiversified management company	An investment company that concentrates its investments among a few issuers or securities and does not meet the diversification requirements of the Investment Company Act of 1940.
nonfixed UIT	A type of UIT that allows changes in the portfolio and traditionally invests in mutual fund shares.
nonqualified retirement plan	A retirement plan that does not allow contributions to be made with pre-tax dollars; that is, the retirement plan does not qualify for beneficial tax treatment from the IRS for its contributions.
nonsystematic risk	A risk that is specific to an issuer or an industry.

note	An intermediate-term interest-bearing security that represents an obligation of its issuer.
not-held (NH) order	An order that gives the floor broker discretion as to the time and price of execution.
numbered account	An account that has been designated a number for identification purposes in order to maintain anonymity for its owner. The owner must sign a statement acknowledging ownership.

O

odd lot	A transaction that is for less than 100 shares of stock or for less than 5 bonds.
odd lot differential	An additional fee that may be charged to an investor for the handling of odd lot transactions (usually waived).
odd lot theory	A contrarian theory that states that small investors will invariably buy and sell at the wrong time.
offer	A price published at which an investor or broker dealer is willing to sell a security.
offering circular	The offering document that is prepared by a corporation selling securities under a Regulation A offering.
office of supervisory jurisdiction (OSJ)	An office identified by the broker dealer as having supervisory responsibilities for agents. It has final approval of new accounts, makes markets, and structures offerings.
Office of the Comptroller of the Currency	An office of the U.S. Treasury that is responsible for regulating the practices of national banks.
official notice of sale	The notice of sale published in the *Daily Bond Buyer* by a municipal issuer that is used to obtain an underwriter for municipal bonds.
official statement	The offering document for a municipal issuer that must be provided to every purchaser if the issuer prepares one.
oil and gas direct participation program	A type of direct participation program designed to invest in oil and gas production or exploration.
oil depletion allowance	An accounting method used to reduce the amount of reserves available from a producing well.
omnibus account	An account used by an introducing member to execute and clear all of its customers' trades.
open-end covenant	A type of bond indenture that allows for the issuance of additional bonds with the same claim on the collateral as the original issue.

open-end investment company	*See* mutual fund.
option	A contract between two investors to purchase or sell a security at a given price for a certain period of time.
option agreement	A form that must be signed and returned by an option investor within 15 days of the account's approval to trade options.
option disclosure document	A document that must be furnished to all option investors at the time the account is approved for options trading. It is published by the Options Clearing Corporation (OCC), and it details the risks and features of standardized options.
Options Clearing Corporation (OCC)	The organization that issues and guarantees the performance of standardized options.
order book official (OBO)	Employees of the CBOE who are responsible for maintaining a fair and orderly market in the options assigned to them and for executing orders that have been left with them.
order department	The department of a broker dealer that is responsible for routing orders to the markets for execution.
order memorandum/ order ticket	The written document filled out by a registered representative that identifies, among other things, the security, the amount, the customer, and the account number for which the order is being entered.
original issue discount (OID)	A bond that has been issued to the public at a discount to its par value. The OID on a corporate bond is taxed as if it was earned annually. The OID on a municipal bond is exempt from taxation.
OTC market	*See* over-the-counter (OTC) market.
out of the money	The relationship of an option's strike price to the underlying security's price when exercising the option would not make economic sense. A call is out of the money when the security's price is below the option's strike price. A put is out of the money when the security's price is above the option's strike price.
outstanding stock	The total amount of a security that has been sold to the investing public and that remains in the hands of the investing public.
overlapping debt	The portion of another taxing authority's debt that a municipality is responsible for.
overriding royalty interest	A type of sharing arrangement that offers an individual with no risk a portion of the revenue in exchange for something of value, such as the right to drill on the owner's land.
over-the-counter (OTC) market	An interdealer market that consists of a computer and phone network through which broker dealers trade securities.

P

par	The stated principal amount of a security. Par value is of great importance for fixed-income securities such as bonds or preferred stock. Par value for bonds is traditionally $1,000, whereas par for a preferred stock is normally $100. Par value is of little importance when looking at common stock.
parity	A condition that results when the value of an underlying common stock to be received upon conversion equals the value of the convertible security.
partial call	A call of a portion of an issuer's callable securities.
participation	The code set forth in the Employee Retirement Income Security Act of 1974 that states who is eligible to participate in an employer sponsored retirement plan.
passive income	Income received by an individual for which no work was performed, such as rental income received from a rental property.
passive loss	A loss realized on an investment in a limited partnership or rental property that can be used to offset passive income.
pass-through certificate	A security that passes through income and principal payments made to an underlying portfolio of mortgages. Ginnie Mae is one of the biggest issuers of this type of security.
payment date	The day when a dividend will actually be sent to investors. The payment date is set by the corporation's board of directors at the time when they initially declare the dividend.
payout stage	The period during which an annuitant receives payments from an annuity contract.
payroll deduction plan	A nonqualified retirement plan where employees authorize the employer to take regular deductions from their paychecks to invest in a retirement account.
pension plan	A contractual retirement plan between an employee and an employer that is designed to provide regular income for the employee after retirement.
percentage depletion	An accounting method that allows for a tax deduction for the reduction of reserves.
periodic payment plan	A contract to purchase mutual fund shares over an extended period of time, usually in exchange for the fund company waiving its minimum investment requirement.
person	Any individual or entity that can enter into a legally binding contract for the purchase and sale of securities.

personal income	Income earned by an individual from providing services and through investments.
phantom income	(1) A term used to describe the taxable appreciation on a zero-coupon bond. (2) The term used to describe taxable income generated by a limited partnership that is not producing positive cash flow.
Philadelphia Automated Communication Execution System (PACE)	The computerized order-routing system for the Philadelphia Stock Exchange.
pink sheets	An electronic quote service containing quotes for unlisted securities that is published by the National Quotation Bureau; operated as the PINK over-the-counter market.
placement ratio	A ratio that details the percentage of municipal bonds sold, relative to the number of bonds offered in the last week, published by the *Daily Bond Buyer*.
plus tick	A transaction in an exchange-listed security that is higher than the previous transaction.
point	An increment of change in the price of a security: 1 bond point equals 1% of par or 1% of $1,000, or $10.
POP	*See* public offering price (POP).
portfolio income	Interest and dividends earned through investing in securities.
portfolio manager	An entity that is hired to manage the investment portfolios of a mutual fund. The portfolio manager is paid a fee that is based on the net assets of the fund.
position	The amount of a security in which an investor has an interest by either being long (owning) or short (owing) the security.
power of substitution	*See* stock power.
preemptive right	The right of a common stockholder to maintain proportional ownership interest in a security. A corporation may not issue additional shares of common stock without first offering those shares to existing stockholders.
preferred stock	An equity security issued with a stated dividend rate. Preferred stockholders have a higher claim on a corporation's dividends and assets than common holders.
preferred stock ratio	A ratio detailing the amount of an issuer's total capitalization that is made up of preferred stock. The ratio is found by dividing the total par value of preferred stock by the issuer's total capitalization.

preliminary prospectus/red herring	A document used to solicit indications of interest during the cooling-off period for a new issue of securities. All of the information in the preliminary prospectus is subject to revision and change. The cover of a preliminary prospectus must have a statement saying that the securities have not yet become registered and that they may not be sold until the registration becomes effective. This statement is written in red ink, and this is where the term *red herring* comes from.
price-earnings ratio (PE)	A measure of value used by analysts. It is calculated by dividing the issuer's stock price by its earnings per share.
price spread	A term used to describe an option spread where the long and short options differ only in their exercise prices.
primary earnings per share	The amount of earnings available per common share prior to the conversion of any outstanding convertible securities.
prime rate	The interest rate that banks charge their best corporate customers on loans.
principal	(1) The face amount of a bond. (2) A broker dealer trading for its own account. (3) An individual who has successfully completed a principal exam and may supervise representatives.
principal transaction	A transaction where a broker dealer participates in a trade by buying or selling securities for its own account.
priority	The acceptance of bids and offers for exchange-listed securities on a first-come, first-served (FCFS) basis.
private placement	The private sale of securities to a limited number of investors. Also known as a Regulation D offering.
profit sharing plan	A plan that allows the employer to distribute a percentage of its profits to its employees at a predetermined rate. The money may be paid directly to the employee or deposited into a retirement account.
progressive tax	A tax structure where the tax rate increases as the income level of the individual or entity increases.
project note	A municipal bond issued as interim financing in anticipation of the issuance of new housing authority bonds.
prospectus	*See* final prospectus.
proxy	A limited authority given by stockholders to another party to vote their shares in a corporate election. The stockholder may specify how the votes are cast or may give the party discretion.
proxy department	The department in a brokerage firm that is responsible for forwarding proxies and financial information to investors whose stock is held in street name.

prudent man rule	A rule that governs investments made by fiduciaries for the benefit of a third party. The rule states that the investments must be similar to those that a prudent person would make for him- or herself.
public offering	The sale of securities by an issuer to public investors.
public offering price (POP)	The price paid by an investor to purchase open-end mutual fund shares. Also the price set for a security the first time it is sold to the investing public.
put	An option contract that allows the buyer to sell a security at a set price for a specific period of time. The seller of a put is obligated to purchase the security at a set price for a specific period of time, should the buyer exercise the option.
put buyer	A bearish investor who pays a premium for the right to sell a security at a set price for a certain period of time.
put spread	An option position created by the simultaneous purchase and sale of two put options on the same underlying security that differ in strike prices, expiration months, or both.
put writer	A bullish investor who sells a put option in order to receive the option premium. The writer is obligated to purchase the security if the buyer exercises the option.

Q

qualified legal opinion	A legal opinion containing conditions or reservations relating to the issue. A legal opinion is issued by a bond counsel for a municipal issuer.
qualified retirement plan	A retirement plan that qualifies for favorable tax treatment by the IRS for contributions made into the plan.
quick assets	A measure of liquidity that subtracts the value of a corporation's unsold inventory from its current assets.
quick ratio	*See* acid-test ratio.
quote	A bid and offer broadcast from the exchange or through the Nasdaq system that displays the prices at which a security may be purchased and sold and in what quantities.

R

range	The price difference between the high and low for a security.

rate covenant	A promise in the trust indenture of a municipal revenue bond to keep the user fees high enough to support the debt service.
rating	A judgment of an issuer's ability to meet its credit obligations. The higher the credit quality of the issuer is, the higher the credit rating. The lower the credit quality is, the lower the credit rating, and the higher the risk associated with the securities.
rating service	Major financial organizations that evaluate the credit quality of issuers. Issuers have to request and pay for the service. Standard and Poor's, Moody's, and Fitch are the most widely followed rating services.
raw land program	A type of real estate limited partnership that invests in land for capital appreciation.
real estate investment trust (REIT)	An entity that is organized to invest in or manage real estate. REITs offer investors certain tax advantages that are beyond the scope of the exam.
real estate limited partnership	A type of direct participation program that invests in real estate projects to produce income or capital appreciation.
real estate mortgage investment conduit (REMIC)	An organization that pools investors' capital to purchase portfolios of mortgages.
realized gain	A profit earned on the sale of a security at a price that exceeds its purchase price.
realized loss	A loss recognized by an investor by selling a security at a price that is less than its purchase price.
reallowance	A sales concession available to dealers who sell securities subject to an offering who are not syndicate or selling group members.
recapture	An event that causes a tax liability on a previously taken deduction, such as selling an asset above its depreciated cost base.
recession	A decline in GDP that lasts for at least 6 months but not longer than 18 months.
reclamation	The right of a seller to demand or claim any loss from the buying party due to the buyer's failure to settle the transaction.
record date	A date set by a corporation's board of directors that determines which shareholders will be entitled to receive a declared dividend. Shareholders must be owners of record on this date in order to collect the dividend.
recourse loan	A loan taken out by a limited partnership that allows the lender to seek payment from the limited partners in the case of the partnership's failure to pay.
redeemable security	A security that can be redeemed by the issuer at the investor's request. Open-end mutual funds are an example of redeemable securities.

redemption	The return of an investor's capital by an issuer. Open-end mutual funds must redeem their securities within 7 days of an investor's request.
red herring	*See* preliminary prospectus.
registered	A term that describes the level of owner information that is recorded by the security's issuer.
registered as to principal only	A type of bond registration that requires the investor to clip coupons to receive the bond's interest payments. The issuer will automatically send the investor the bond's principal amount at maturity.
registered options principal (ROP)	An individual who has passed the Series 4 exam.
registered principal	A supervisor of a member firm who has passed the principal examination.
registered representative	An individual who has successfully completed a qualified examination to represent a broker dealer or issuer in securities transactions.
registrar	An independent organization that accounts for all outstanding stock and bonds of an issuer.
registration statement	The full disclosure statement that nonexempt issuers must file with the SEC prior to offering securities for sale to the public. The Securities Act of 1933 requires that a registration statement be filed.
regressive tax	A tax that is levied on all parties at the same rate, regardless of their income. An example of a regressive tax is a sales tax. A larger percentage of a low-income earner's income is taken away by the tax.
regular-way settlement	The standard number of business days in which a securities transaction is completed and paid for. Corporate securities and municipal bonds settle the regular way on the second business day after the trade date with payment due on the fourth business day. Government securities settle the next business day.
regulated investment company	An investment company that qualifies as a conduit for net investment income under Internal Revenue Code subchapter M, so long as it distributes at least 90% of its net investment income to shareholders.
Regulation A	A small company offering that allows a company to raise up to $5 million in any 12-month period, without filing a full registration.
Regulation D	A private placement or sale of securities that allows for an exemption from registration under the Securities Act of 1933. A private placement may be sold to an unlimited number of accredited investors but may only be sold to 35 nonaccredited investors in any 12-month period.
Regulation G	Regulates the extension of credit for securities purchases by other commercial lenders.

Regulation T	Regulates the extension of credit by broker dealers for securities purchases.
Regulation U	Regulates the extension of credit by banks for securities purchases.
Regulation X	Regulates the extension of credit by overseas lenders for securities purchases.
Rehypothecation	The act of a broker dealer repledging a customer's securities as collateral at a bank to obtain a loan for the customer.
REIT	*See* real estate investment trust (REIT).
rejection	The act of a buyer of a security refusing delivery.
reorganization department	The department in a brokerage firm that handles changes in securities that result from a merger or acquisition or calls.
repurchase agreement (REPO)	A fully collateralized loan that results in a sale of securities to the lender, with the borrower agreeing to repurchase them at a higher price in the future. The higher price represents the lender's interest.
reserve maintenance fund	An account set up to provide additional funds to maintain a revenue-producing facility financed by a revenue bond.
reserve requirement	A deposit required to be placed on account with the Federal Reserve Board by banks. The requirement is a percentage of the bank's customers' deposits.
resistance	A price level to which a security appreciates and attracts sellers. The new sellers keep the security's price from rising any higher.
restricted account	(1) A long margin account that has less than 50% equity but more than 25%. (2) A customer account that has been subject to a sellout.
restricted stock	A nonexempt unregistered security that has been obtained by means other than a public offering.
retail communication	Any communication that may be seen in whole or in part by an individual investor. Retail communication must be approved by a principal prior to first use and maintained by the firm for 3 years.
retained earnings	The amount of a corporation's net income that has not been paid out to shareholders as dividends.
retention	The amount of a new issue that an underwriter allocates to its own clients.
retention requirement	The amount of equity that must be left in a restricted margin account when withdrawing securities.
return on equity	A measure of performance found by dividing after-tax income by common stockholders' equity.
return on investment (ROI)	The profit or loss realized by an investor from holding a security expressed as a percentage of the invested capital.
revenue anticipation note	A short-term municipal issue that is sold to manage an issuer's cash flow in anticipation of other revenue in the future.

reverse repurchase agreement	A fully collateralized loan that results in the purchase of securities with the intention of reselling them to the borrower at a higher price. The higher price represents the buyer's/lender's interest.
reverse split	A stock split that results in fewer shares outstanding, with each share being worth proportionally more.
reversionary working interest	A revenue-sharing arrangement where the general partner shares none of the cost and receives none of the revenue until the limited partners have received their payments back, plus any predetermined amount of return.
right	A short-term security issued in conjunction with a shareholder's preemptive right. The maximum length of a right is 45 days, and it is issued with a subscription price, which allows the holder to purchase the underlying security at a discount from its market price.
rights agent	An independent entity responsible for maintaining the records for rights holders.
rights of accumulation	A right offered to mutual fund investors that allows them to calculate all past contributions and growth to reach a breakpoint to receive a sales charge discount on future purchases.
rights offering	The offering of new shares by a corporation that is preceded by the offering of the new shares to existing shareholders.
riskless simultaneous transaction	The purchase of a security on a principal basis by a brokerage firm for the sole purpose of filling a customer's order that the firm has already received. The markup on riskless principal transactions has to be based on the firm's actual cost for the security.
rollover	The distribution of assets from a qualified account to an investor for the purpose of depositing the assets in another qualified account within 60 days. An investor may only roll over an IRA once every 12 months.
round lot	A standard trading unit for securities. For common and preferred stock, a round lot is 100 shares. For bonds, it is 5 bonds.
Rule 144	SEC rule that regulates the sale of restricted and control securities requiring the seller to file Form 144 at the time the order is entered to sell. Rule 144 also regulates the number of securities that may be sold.
Rule 145	SEC rule that requires a corporation to provide stockholders with full disclosure relating to reorganizations and to solicit proxies.
Rule 147	An intrastate offering that provides an exemption from SEC registration.
Rule 405	The NYSE rule that requires that all customer recommendations must be suitable and that the representative must "know" the customer.

S

sale	*See* sell.
sales charge	*See* commission.
sales literature	Written material distributed by a firm to a controlled audience for the purpose of increasing business. Sales literature includes market letters, research reports, and form letters sent to more than 25 customers.
sales load	The amount of commission charged to investors in open-end mutual funds. The amount of the sales load is added to the net asset value of the fund to determine the public offering price of the fund.
satellite office	An office not identified to the public as an office of the member, such as an agent's home office.
savings bond	A nonnegotiable U.S. government bond that must be purchased from the government and redeemed to the government. These bonds are generally known as Series EE and HH bonds.
scale	A list of maturities and yields for a new serial bond issue.
Schedule 13D	A form that must be filed with the SEC by any individual or group of individuals acquiring 5% or more of a corporation's nonexempt equity securities. Form 13D must be filed within 10 days of the acquisition.
scheduled premium policy	A variable life insurance policy with fixed premium payments.
SEC	*See* Securities and Exchange Commission (SEC).
secondary distribution	A distribution of a large number of securities by a large shareholder or group of large shareholders. The distribution may or may not be done under a prospectus.
secondary offering	An underwriting of a large block of stock being sold by large shareholders. The proceeds of the issue are received by the selling shareholders, not the corporation.
secondary market	A marketplace where securities are exchanged between investors. All transactions that take place on an exchange or on the Nasdaq are secondary market transactions.
sector fund	A mutual fund that invests in companies within a specific business area in an effort to maximize gains. Sector funds have larger risk-reward ratios because of the concentration of investments.
Securities Act of 1933	The first major piece of securities industry legislation. It regulates the primary market and requires that nonexempt issuers file a registration statement

with the SEC. The act also requires that investors in new issues be given a prospectus.

Securities Act Amendments of 1975	Created the Municipal Securities Rulemaking Board (MSRB).
Securities Exchange Act of 1934	Regulates the secondary market and all broker dealers and industry participants. It created the Securities and Exchange Commission, the industry's ultimate authority. The act gave the authority to the Federal Reserve Board to regulate the extension of credit for securities purchases through Regulation T.
Securities and Exchange Commission	The ultimate securities industry authority. The SEC is a direct government body, not a self-regulatory organization. The commissioners are appointed by the U.S. President and must be approved by Congress.
Securities Investor Protection Corporation (SIPC)	The industry's nonprofit insurance company that provides protection for investors in case of broker dealer failure. All member firms must pay dues to SIPC based upon their revenue. SIPC provides coverage for each separate customer for up to $500,000, of which a maximum of $250,000 may be cash. The Securities Investor Protection Act of 1970 created SIPC.
security	Any investment that can be exchanged for value between two parties that contains risk. Securities include stocks, bonds, mutual funds, notes, rights, warrants, and options, among others.
segregation	The physical separation of customer and firm assets.
self-regulatory organization (SRO)	An industry authority that regulates its own members. FINRA, the NYSE, and the CBOE are all self-regulatory organizations that regulate their own members.
sell	The act of conveying the ownership of a security for value to another party. A sale includes any security that is attached to another security, as well as any security which the security may be converted or exchanged into.
seller's option	A type of settlement option that allows the seller to determine when delivery of the securities and final settlement of the trade will occur.
selling away	Any recommendation to a customer that involves an investment product that is not offered through the employing firm without the firm's knowledge and consent. This is a violation of industry regulations and may result in action being taken against the representative.
selling concession	*See* concession.
selling dividends	The act of using a pending dividend to create urgency for the customer to purchase a security. This is a violation and could result in action being taken against the representative.

selling group	A group of broker dealers who may sell a new issue of securities but who are not members of the syndicate and who have no liability to the issuer.
sell out	A transaction executed by a broker dealer when a customer fails to pay for the securities.
sell-stop order	An order placed beneath the current market for a security to protect a profit, to guard against a loss, or to establish a short position.
separate account	The account established by an insurance company to invest the pooled funds of variable contract holders in the securities markets. The separate account must register as either an open-end investment company or as a unit investment trust.
separate trading of registered interest and principal securities (STRIPS)	A zero-coupon bond issued by the U.S. government. The principal payment due in the future is sold to investors at a discount and appreciates to par at maturity. The interest payment component is sold to other investors who want some current income.
serial bonds	A bond issue that has an increasing amount of principal maturing in successive years.
Series EE bond	A nonmarketable U.S. government zero-coupon bond that is issued at a discount and matures at its face value. Investors must purchase the bonds from the U.S. government and redeem them to the government at maturity.
Series HH bond	A nonmarketable U.S. government interest-bearing bond that can only be purchased by trading in matured Series EE bonds. Series HH bonds may not be purchased with cash and are issued with a $500 minimum denomination.
settlement	The completion of a securities transaction. A transaction settles and is completed when the security is delivered to the buyer and the cash is delivered to the seller.
settlement date	The date when a securities ownership changes. Settlement dates are set by FINRA's Uniform Practice Code.
75-5-10 diversification	The diversification test that must be met by mutual funds under the Investment Company Act of 1940 in order to market themselves as a diversified mutual fund: 75% of the fund's assets must be invested in other issuer's securities, no more than 5% of the fund's assets may be invested in any one company, and the fund may own no more than 10% of an issuer's outstanding securities.
shareholder's equity	*See* net worth.
share identification	The process of identifying which shares are being sold at the time the sale order is entered in order to minimize an investor's tax liability.

shelf offering	A type of securities registration that allows the issuer to sell the securities over a 2-year period.
short	A position established by a bearish investor that is created by borrowing the security and selling in the hopes that the price of the security will fall. The investor hopes to be able to repurchase the security at a lower price, thus replacing it cheaply. If the security's price rises, the investor will suffer a loss.
short against the box	A short position established against an equal long position in the security to roll tax liabilities forward. Most of the benefits of establishing a short against the box position have been eliminated.
short straddle	The simultaneous sale of a call and a put on the same underlying security with the same strike price and expiration. A short straddle would be established by an investor who believes that the security price will move sideways.
simplified arbitration	A method of resolving disputes of $50,000 or less. There is no hearing; one arbitrator reads the submissions and renders a final decision.
Simplified Employee Pension (SEP)	A qualified retirement plan created for small employers with 25 or fewer employees that allows the employees' money to grow tax-deferred until retirement.
single account	An account operated for one individual. The individual has control of the account, and the assets go to the individual's estate in the case of his or her death.
sinking fund	An account established by an issuer of debt to place money for the exclusive purpose of paying bond principal.
special assessment bond	A municipal bond backed by assessments from the property that benefits from the improvements.
specialist	Member of an exchange responsible for maintaining a fair and orderly market in the securities that he or she specializes in and for executing orders left with him or her.
specialist book	A book of limit orders left with the specialist for execution.
special situation fund	A fund that seeks to take advantage of unusual corporate developments, such as take mergers and restructuring.
special tax bond	A type of municipal revenue bond that is supported only by revenue from certain taxes.
speculation	An investment objective where the investor is willing to accept a high degree of risk in exchange for the opportunity to realize a high return.
split offering	An offering where a portion of the proceeds from the underwriting goes to the issuer and a portion goes to the selling shareholders.

spousal account	An IRA opened for a nonworking spouse that allows a full contribution to be made for the nonworking spouse.
spread	(1) The difference between the bid and ask for a security. (2) The simultaneous purchase and sale of two calls or two puts on the same underlying security.
spread load plan	A contractual plan that seeks to spread the sales charge over a longer period of time, as detailed in the Spread Load Plan Act of 1970. The maximum sales charge over the life of the plan is 9%, while the maximum sales charge in any one year is 20%.
stabilizing	The only form of price manipulation allowed by the SEC. The managing underwriter enters a bid at or below the offering price to ensure even distribution of shares.
standby underwriting	An underwriting used in connection with a preemptive rights offering. The standby underwriter must purchase any shares not subscribed to by existing shareholders.
statutory disqualification	A set of rules that prohibit an individual who has been barred or suspended or convicted of a securities-related crime from becoming registered.
statutory voting	A method of voting that requires investors to cast their votes evenly for the directors they wish to elect.
stock ahead	A condition that causes an investor's order not to be executed, even though the stock is trading at a price that would satisfy the customer's limit order, because other limit orders have been entered prior to the customer's order.
stock certificate	Evidence of equity ownership.
stock or bond power	A form that, when signed by the owner and attached to a security, makes the security negotiable.
stock split	A change in the number of outstanding shares, the par value, and the number of authorized shares that has been approved through a vote of the shareholders. Forward-stock splits increase the number of shares outstanding and reduce the stock price in order to make the security more attractive to individual investors.
stop limit order	An order that becomes a limit order to buy or sell the stock when the stock trades at or through the stop price.
stop order	An order that becomes a market order to buy or sell the stock when the stock trades at or through the stop price.
stopping stock	A courtesy offered by a specialist to public customers, whereby the specialist guarantees a price but tries to obtain a better price for the customer.
straddle	The simultaneous purchase or sale of a call and a put on the same security with the same strike price and expiration.

straight line depreciation	An accounting method that allows an owner to take equal tax deductions over the useful life of the asset.
strangle	The purchase or sale of a call and a put on either side of the current market price. The options have the same expiration months but different strike prices.
stripped bond	A bond that has had its coupons removed by a broker dealer and that is selling at a deep discount to its principal payment in the future.
stripper well	An oil well that is in operation just to recover a very limited amount of reserves.
subchapter S corporation	A business organization that allows the tax consequences of the organization to flow through to the owners.
subscription agreement	An application signed by the purchaser of an interest in a direct participation plan. An investor in a limited partnership does not become an investor until the general partner signs the subscription agreement.
subscription right	*See* right.
suitability	A determination that the characteristics of a security are in line with an investor's objectives, financial profile, and attitudes.
Super Display Book System (SDBK)	The electronic order-routing system used by the NYSE to route orders directly to the trading post.
supervise	The actions of a principal that ensure that the actions of a firm and its representatives are in compliance with industry regulations.
support	The price to which a security will fall and attract new buyers. As the new buyers enter the market, it keeps the price from falling any lower.
surplus fund	An account set up for funds generated by a project financed by a municipal revenue bond to pay a variety of expenses.
syndicate	A group of underwriters responsible for underwriting a new issue.
systematic risk	A risk inherent in any investment in the market. An investor may lose money simply because the market is going down.

T

takedown	The price at which a syndicate purchases a new issue of securities from the issuer.
tax and revenue anticipation note	A short-term note sold by a municipal issuer as interim financing in anticipation of tax and other revenue.

tax anticipation note (TAN)	A short-term note sold by a municipal issuer as interim financing in anticipation of tax revenue.
tax-deferred annuity	A nonqualified retirement account that allows an investor's money to grow tax deferred. A tax-deferred annuity is a contract between an insurance company and an investor.
tax equivalent yield	The interest rate that must be offered by a taxable bond of similar quality in order to be equal to the rate that is offered by a municipal bond.
tax-exempt bond fund	A bond fund that seeks to produce investment income that is free from federal tax by investing in a portfolio of municipal bonds.
tax liability	The amount of money that is owed by an investor after realizing a gain on the sale of an investment or after receiving investment income.
tax preference item	An item that receives preferential tax treatment and must be added back into income when calculating an investor's alternative minimum tax.
tax-sheltered annuity (TSA)	A qualified retirement plan offered to employees of governments, school systems, or nonprofit organizations. Contributions to TSAs are made with pre-tax dollars.
technical analysis	A method of security analysis that uses past price performance to predict the future performance of a security.
Telephone Consumer Protection Act of 1991	Legislation that regulates how potential customers are contacted by phone at home.
tenants in common	*See* joint tenants in common.
tender offer	An offer to buy all or part of a company's outstanding securities for cash or cash and securities.
term bond	A bond issue that has its entire principal due on one date.
term maturity	A type of bond maturity that has all principal due on one date.
testimonial	The use of a recognized expert or leader to endorse the services of a firm.
third market	A transaction in an exchange-listed security executed over the Nasdaq workstation.
third-party account	An account that is managed for the benefit of a customer by another party, such as an investment adviser, a trustee, or an attorney.
30-day visible supply	The total par value of all new issue municipal bonds coming to market in the next 30 days.
time deposit	An account that is established by a bank customer where the customer agrees to leave the funds on deposit for an agreed upon amount of time.

time value	The value of an option that exceeds its intrinsic value or its in-the-money amount.
tombstone ad	An announcement published in financial papers advertising the offering of securities by a group of underwriters. Only basic information may be contained in the tombstone ad, and all offers must be made through the prospectus only.
top heavy rule	The rule that states the maximum salary for which a Keogh contribution may be based. This is in effect to limit the disparity between high- and low-salary employees.
trade confirmation	The printed notification of a securities transaction. A confirmation must be sent to a customer on or before the completion of a transaction. The completion of a transaction is considered to be the settlement date.
trade date	The day when an investor's order is executed.
tranche	A class of collateralized mortgage obligation (CMO) that has a predicted maturity and interest rate.
transfer agent	An independent entity that handles name changes, records the names of security holders of record, and ensures that all certificates are properly endorsed.
transfer and hold in safekeeping	A request by customers for the brokerage firm to transfer their securities into the firm's name and to hold them in safekeeping at the firm. A brokerage may charge a fee for holding a customer's securities that have been registered in its name.
transfer and ship	A request by customers for the brokerage firm to transfer their securities into their name and to ship them to their address of record.
Treasury bill	A U.S. government security that is issued at a discount and matures at par in 4, 13, 26, and 52 weeks.
Treasury bond	A long-term U.S. government security that pays semiannual interest and matures in 10 to 30 years.
Treasury note	An intermediate-term U.S. government security that pays semiannual interest and matures in 1 to 10 years.
Treasury receipt	A zero-coupon bond created by a brokerage firm that is backed by U.S. government securities. It is issued at a discount and matures at par.
treasury stock	Stock that has been issued by a corporation and that has subsequently been repurchased by the corporation. Treasury stock does not vote or receive dividends. It is not used in the calculation of earnings per share.
trendline	A line used to predict the future price movement for a security. Drawing a line under the successive lows or successive highs creates a trendline.

trough	The bottoming out of the business cycle just prior to an new upward movement in activity.
true interest cost (TIC)	A calculation for the cost of a municipal issuer's interest expense that includes the time value of money.
Trust Indenture Act of 1940	Regulates the issuance of corporate debt in excess of $5 million and with a term exceeding 1 year. It requires an indenture between the issuer and the trustee.
trustee	A person who legally acts for the benefit of another party.
12B-1 fee	An asset-based distribution fee that is assessed annually and paid out quarterly to cover advertising and distribution costs. All 12B-1 fees must be reasonable.
two-dollar broker	An independent exchange member who executes orders for commission house brokers and other customers for a fee.
type	A classification method for an option as either a call or a put.

U

uncovered	*See* naked.
underlying security	A security for which an investor has an option to buy or sell.
underwriting	The process of marketing a new issue of securities to the investing public. A broker dealer forwards the proceeds of the sale to the issuer minus its fee for selling the securities.
unearned income	Any income received by an individual from an investment, such as dividends and interest income.
uniform delivery ticket	A document that must be attached to every security delivered by the seller, making the security "good delivery."
Uniform Gifts to Minors Act (UGMA)	Sets forth guidelines for the gifting of cash and securities to minors and for the operation of accounts managed for the benefit of minors. Once a gift is given to a minor, it is irrevocable.
Uniform Practice Code	The FINRA bylaw that sets guidelines for how industry members transact business with other members. The Uniform Practice Code establishes such things as settlement dates, rules of good delivery, and ex-dividend dates.
Uniform Securities Act (USA)	The framework for state-based securities legislation. The act is a model that can be adapted to each state's particular needs.

Uniform Transfer to Minors Act (UTMA)	Legislation that has been adopted in certain states, in lieu of the Uniform Gifts to Minors Act. UTMA allows the custodian to determine the age at which the assets become the property of the minor. The maximum age for transfer of ownership is 25.
unit investment trust (UIT)	A type of investment company organized as a trust to invest in a portfolio of securities. The UIT sells redeemable securities to investors in the form of shares or units of beneficial interest.
unit of beneficial interest	The redeemable share issued to investors in a unit investment trust.
unit refund annuity	An annuity payout option that will make payments to the annuitant for life. If the annuitant dies prior to receiving an amount that is equal to his or her account value, the balance of the account will be paid to the annuitant's beneficiaries.
unqualified legal opinion	A legal opinion issued by a bond attorney for the issue where there are no reservations relating to the issue.
unrealized	A paper profit or loss on a security that is still owned.

V

variable annuity	A contract issued by an insurance company that is both a security and an insurance product. The annuitant's contributions are invested through the separate account into a portfolio of securities. The annuitant's payments depend largely on the investment results of the separate account.
variable death benefit	The amount of a death benefit paid to a beneficiary that is based on the investment results of the insurance company's separate account. This amount is over the contract's minimum guaranteed death benefit.
variable life insurance	A life insurance policy that provides for a minimum guaranteed death benefit, as well as an additional death benefit, based on the investment results of the separate account.
variable rate municipal security	Interim municipal financing issued with a variable rate.
vertical spread	The simultaneous purchase and sale of two calls or two puts on the same underlying security that differ only in strike price.
vesting	The process by which an employer's contributions to an employee's retirement account become the property of the employee.
visible supply	*See* 30-day visible supply.

voluntary accumulation plan	A method, such as dollar-cost averaging, by which an investor regularly makes contributions to acquire mutual fund shares.
voting right	The right of a corporation's stockholders to cast their votes for the election of the corporation's board of directors as well as for certain major corporate issues.

W

warrant	A long-term security that gives the holder the right to purchase the common shares of a corporation for up to 10 years. The warrant's subscription price is always higher than the price of the underlying common shares when the warrant is initially issued.
wash sale	The sale of a security at a loss and the subsequent repurchase of that security or of a security that is substantially the same within 30 days of the sale. The repurchase disallows the claim of the loss for tax purposes.
western account	A type of municipal security syndicate account where only the member with unsold bonds is responsible for the unsold bonds.
when-issued security	A security that has been sold prior to the certificates being available for delivery.
wildcatting	An exploratory oil- and gas-drilling program.
wire room	*See* order department.
withdrawal plan	The systematic removal of funds from a mutual fund account over time. Withdrawal plans vary in type and availability among fund companies.
workable indication	An indication of the prices and yields that a municipal securities dealer may be willing to buy or sell bonds.
working capital	A measure of a corporation's liquidity that is found by subtracting current liabilities from current assets.
working interest	An interest that requires the holder to bear the proportional expenses and allows the holder to share in the revenue produced by an oil or gas project in relation to the interest.
workout quote	A nonfirm quote that requires handling and settlement conditions to be worked out between the parties prior to the trade.
writer	An investor who sells an option to receive the premium income.
writing the scale	The procedure of assigning prospective yields to a new issuer of serial municipal bonds.

Y

Yellow Sheets	A daily publication published by the national quotation bureau providing quotes for corporate bonds.
yield	The annual amount of income generated by a security relative to its price; expressed as a percentage.
yield-based option	An interest rate option that allows the holder to receive the in-the-money amount in cash upon exercise or expiration.
yield curve	The rate at which interest rates vary among investments of similar quality with different maturities. Longer-term securities generally offer higher yields.
yield to call	An investor's overall return for owning a bond should it be called in prior to maturity by the issuer.
yield to maturity	An investor's overall return for owning a bond if the bond is held until maturity.

Z

zero-coupon bond	A bond that is issued at a discount from its par value and makes no regular interest payments. An investor's interest is reflected by the security's appreciation toward par at maturity. The appreciation is taxable each year even though it is not actually received by the investor (phantom income).
zero-minus tick	A trade in an exchange-listed security that occurs at the same price as the previous transaction, but at a price that is lower than the last transaction that was different.
zero-plus tick	A trade in an exchange-listed security that occurs at the same price as the previous transaction, but at a price that is higher than the last transaction that was different.

Y

Yellow Sheets   A daily publication published by the National Quotation Bureau providing quotes on corporate bonds.

yield   The total amount of income generated relative to a certain value relative to its price, expressed as a percentage.

yield-based option   An index of rate option that allows the holder to receive the cash-settlement amount in cash upon exercise or expiration.

yield curve   The rate at which interest rates vary among investments of similar quality with different maturities. Longer term securities usually offer higher yields.

yield to call   An investor's yield if a security or bond should be called prior to maturity to the buyer.

yield to maturity   An investor's overall return for owning a bond if the bond is held until maturity.

Z

zero-coupon bond   A bond that is issued at a discount and has no interest value but makes no regular interest payments. An investor's interest is reflected by the security's appreciation toward par at maturity. The appreciation is taxable each year even though it is not actually received by the investor as phantom income.

zero-minus tick   A trade in an exchange-listed security that occurs at the same price as the previous transaction but at a price that is lower than the last transaction that was different.

zero-plus tick   A trade in an exchange-listed security that occurs at the same price as the previous transaction but at a price that is higher than the last transaction that was different.

Index